Hmo
12

More than PETTICOATS

Remarkable Montana Women

D1051927

Gayle C. Shirley

TWODOT

For Joan Shirley,

a remarkable Montana woman

in her own right

A · TWODOT · BOOK

© 1995 by Falcon Press Publishing Co., Inc.,
Helena and Billings, Montana.
Reprinted in 1996.

Cover photo by Evelyn Cameron, courtesy of Montana Historical Society, Helena

All rights reserved, including the right to reproduce this book or any parts thereof in any form, except brief quotations in a review.

Design, typesetting, and other prepress work by Falcon Press, Helena, Montana.

Printed in U.S.A.

Library of Congress Cataloging-in-Publication Data

Shirley, Gayle Corbett.
    More than petticoats : remarkable Montana women / Gayle C.
Shirley.
        p.   cm.
    Includes bibliographical references and index.
    Contents: Pretty Shield -- Lucia Darling Park -- Mattie Castner --
Helen Clarke -- Mother Amadeus -- Mary Fields -- Maria Dean -- Ella
Knowles Haskell -- Evelyn Cameron -- Fra Dana -- Fanny Cory Cooney -
- Nancy Cooper Russell -- Fanny Sperry Steele -- Jeannette Rankin.
    ISBN 1-56044-363-4
    1. Women--Montana--Biography. 2. Montana--Biography. I. Title.
CT3260.S455 1995
920.72'09786--dc20   95-32881
                                                            CIP

There are unwritten chapters in the history of every new settlement, which no pen will ever write, but could they be written, they would tell of many heroines as well as heroes, women as brave and deserving of credit as those who landed from the Mayflower. They have had much to do in "winning the west," and a higher civilization has always followed closely in the footsteps of the woman pioneer.

Lucia Darling Park
1839-1905

$\mathcal{A}$CKNOWLEDGMENTS

$\mathcal{I}$'d like to thank the following people, who shared their knowledge and expertise, guided me in my research, and/or critiqued parts of the manuscript for accuracy:

* Flora Abernathy, reference librarian at the Catawba County Historical Museum Library, Newton, North Carolina.
* Sister Elisabeth Marie Charvet, O.S.U., archivist at the Ursuline Centre, Great Falls, Montana.
* Bob Clark and Dorothea Simonson, reference librarians at the Montana Historical Society, Helena.
* Mr. and Mrs. Robert Cooney, Helena.
* Liz Dear, curator of the C. M. Russell Museum, Great Falls.
* Ethel Castner Kennedy, Belt, Montana.
* Dennis Kern, curator of the University of Montana Museum of Fine Arts, Missoula.
* Wendell F. Lauth, past president of the Trumbull County Historical Society, Bristolville, Ohio.
* Mary Murphy, assistant professor of history, Montana State University, Bozeman.
* Joyce Clarke Turvey, East Glacier, Montana.

Finally, I'd especially like to thank my husband, Steve, for his loving and constructive editing; Dave Walter, research historian, for thoroughly reviewing the entire manuscript; and Megan Hiller, my editor, for her moral support, helpful suggestions, and incredible patience.

Contents

Introduction

According to an old axiom, women *are* history, but men *make* history. That certainly seemed to be the case for all too many generations. For two centuries after our forefathers gave birth to our nation, presumably without the help of foremothers, every American schoolchild studied a history made up mostly of kings, presidents, emperors, generals, and the wars they waged among themselves. History books were packed with patrilineal family trees, colorful maps of fluctuating borders, and elaborate battle plans in which blue squares represented the good guys and red squares the bad.

Then, in the 1960s and 1970s, American women did make history. In the course of what became known as the feminist revolution, they demanded recognition of their value and contributions—today, tomorrow, and yesterday. In the two decades since, historians have begun taking a serious look at the role women played in the building of our nation. Eventually they trained their microscopes on women of the West—those who came by steamboat, train, and covered wagon and those who were already here.

At first, scholars shuffled western women into convenient pigeonholes. There was the idealized "madonna of the prairies," a long-suffering pioneer wife and mother who gamely toiled across the Great Plains in calico and sunbonnet. There was the disreputable "soiled dove," an enterprising floozy who made her living in hurdy-gurdys and houses of ill repute. And there were the maiden schoolmarms, the servile "squaws," and the pistol-packing Calamity Janes.

But as historians unearthed letters and diaries left behind by flesh-and-blood frontier women, and as they learned more about the Native American and Hispanic women who were here before, they discovered that there are no convenient stereotypes. The women of the Old West were as diverse as boulders in the badlands. They came from different backgrounds, had different experiences, and responded to frontier conditions in different ways.

For some of them, the move West was like taking off a corset—they were finally able to breathe. The frontier offered them new opportunities to express their individuality. For others, the West was a land of privation and hardship where the struggle to survive overrode other desires. And for still others, the West was simply an extension of the East. They brought with them all the repressive baggage of the "cult of true womanhood," which demanded that they be pious, pure, submissive, and domestic.

"If there is a truth about frontierswomen," one author contended, "it is that they were not any one thing."

This wealth of diversity is apparent in the following pages, which celebrate fourteen remarkable women who made their mark on Montana history.

One hazard inherent in writing about the past is the tendency to view historical events from a contemporary perspective. Yet, how can we do otherwise? We're all products of our times. Values and attitudes change, and what may have been socially acceptable a century ago may not now be "politically correct." This is especially apparent with regard to women and minorities—the subjects of this book.

I've tried to keep modern sensibilities in mind as I've written *More Than Petticoats*—but not at the expense of historical accuracy. For how can we judge how far we've come if we refuse to acknowledge where we've been? The fact is, women and minorities were considered inferior a century ago, and that attitude is apparent in some of the quotations I've used in this book. That we know better today doesn't mean it's our job to erase incidents of sexism and racism from our history books and pretend they never existed. Our responsibility, I believe, is to recognize them for what they were and demonstrate with our own behavior that civilization has made progress.

When I originally began work on this book, my first challenge was to identify a dozen or so women worthy of inclusion. At first, I feared I would never find enough. But as I dug into the archives of the state historical society, I developed a new worry. How was I to decide which of countless fascinating Montana women to include? How could I be sure I didn't overlook someone important?

To keep the book a manageable size, I arbitrarily chose to limit it to women born before 1900, thereby giving the hook to such famous Montanans as actress Myrna Loy and author Dorothy Johnson. I also tried to choose a cross section of women who excelled in various fields—from doctor, lawyer, and teacher to entrepreneur and rodeo queen. Finally, I sought out interesting and inspiring women of all races and ethnicities and aimed for balance.

I'm sure readers will be able to think of others who deserve to be featured in this book but aren't. I regret leaving any of those women out. The fact is, all of the women who helped to forge Montana were remarkable—those who tirelessly pounded animal hides into supple leather to clothe their families; those who waited out blizzards in home-steader shacks; those who packed lunch pails for husbands headed to the mines; those who raised money to build churches, schools, and libraries.

They were all heroines. They all helped make Montana what it is today. ⚜

MONTANA HISTORICAL SOCIETY, HELENA

Pretty Shield

Pretty Shield

Crow Healer

*F*our days had passed since the birth of Kills In The Night's fourth child. But in the eyes of the Crows, the infant was still a nobody because she had not yet been given a name. It was March, and as the icy crust of the Missouri River began to melt, that was about to change. In keeping with Crow tradition, the child's paternal grandfather, Little Boy Strikes With A Lance, had announced that he was ready to name his granddaughter.

Kills In The Night bundled her newborn baby in buckskin to protect her from the last bite of winter, and with her husband, Crazy Sister In Law, by her side, she proudly carried the infant to the old man's lodge. Little Boy Strikes With A Lance sat before a small fire at the center of his tepee. As he took the child in his hands, one of his family dropped chips of dried bear-root into the flames, creating a sweet-smelling smoke that climbed lazily toward the lodge's smoke hole.

Little Boy Strikes With A Lance held his granddaughter on his palms in the midst of the purifying smoke and began to chant a prayer. "May this child grow to be healthy," he sang as he lifted her four times toward the heavens. Then he presented her with her name:

Pretty Shield, in honor of his handsome war shield, half red and half blue, which hung on a tripod behind his lodge. The child would grow to be one of the most respected members of her tribe, a great healer of body and spirit.

No record exists of Pretty Shield's birth, but she once claimed that she was born in "the snow that Yellow-calf and his war-party were wiped out by the Lacota [Sioux]," probably in the late 1850s. Yet, much is known about the rest of her life, which is surprising because the Crows preserved their history orally rather than in writing, and because for many years few historians or scholars were interested in what they perceived to be the dreary lives of Native American women.

One exception was Frank Bird Linderman, a Chicago native who came to Montana at the age of sixteen and spent the next forty years studying and writing about the Plains Indians. Two of his best-known books were the result of interviews with Pretty Shield and with the great Crow chief Plenty Coups. The latter gave Linderman his Crow name, Mah-paht-sa-mot-tsasa, or Great Sign Talker.

Using sign language and an interpreter, Linderman interviewed Pretty Shield in the early 1930s, when Crow Agency records indicated that she was seventy-four years old. He was pleasantly surprised when she agreed to talk to him. He explained why in the foreword of her biography.

> Throughout forty-six years in Montana I have had much to do with its several Indian tribes, and yet never, until now, talked for ten consecutive minutes directly to an old Indian woman. I have found Indian women diffident, and so self-effacing that acquaintance with them is next to impossible. . . . I had nearly given up the idea of ever writing the life of an old Indian woman when Pretty-

shield delighted me by consenting to tell me her story.

Of all the old Indian women I know Pretty-shield would have been my choice, since in her the three essential qualifications for such story telling are in happy combination: age that permits her to have known the natural life of her people on the plains, keen mentality, and, above all, the willingness to talk to me without restraint. Besides these necessary qualifications Pretty-shield is a "Wise-one," a medicine-woman, of the Crow tribe.

As she spoke to Linderman, Pretty Shield was reluctant to discuss her later years, after the buffalo had disappeared from the plains and the hearts of the Crows had, in her words, "turned to stone." She dwelt, instead, on her childhood—a carefree and happy time spent playing many of the same games enjoyed by children of other cultures. She told of kicking a ball made by stuffing antelope hair into the thin sac of skin that had surrounded a buffalo's heart. She skimmed down snowy hillsides on a sled fashioned from buffalo ribs. And sometimes she and her friends transformed themselves into "mud clowns" and entertained their village with song and dance.

Like children everywhere, Pretty Shield sometimes succumbed to mischief. She and a friend once sneaked around the village in the night, pulling the poles out of the tepees' smoke-ears so that they flapped closed and the lodges filled with smoke. On another occasion, she and her friend stole a shield and tobacco pouch from the burial lodge of a dead Sioux warrior. Her father found out and punished her. He didn't spank her—Crow parents didn't strike their children—but he made her return the objects and gave her a stern lecture. "Ah, how my father talked to me that time!" she recalled. "And I needed to be talked to."

Sometime before Pretty Shield turned three, her aunt Strikes With An Axe lost her husband and two daughters when their village was attacked by Sioux. The young woman mourned for so long and grew so thin and weak that Kills In The Night gave her Pretty Shield, with the hope that the child would help to heal her heart. Pretty Shield moved to her aunt's village, but because the various Crow clans rendezvoused often, she still had many opportunities to see her mother. She didn't seem to mind the separations. She told Linderman that she was happy in her aunt's large lodge, perhaps even happier than she would have been at home, because she knew her aunt needed her.

Unlike white children, Indian youngsters didn't attend school. Instead, they learned about their culture in other ways, often by imitating their elders. Boys played at war and raced each other on horseback. Girls played house and mothered their dolls. Pretty Shield told of carrying her doll on her back like a Crow mother and of pitching her own small tepee, hurrying to get a fire going inside it before her aunt could kindle one in her own lodge. Groups of girls would construct play villages, pretending their dolls were children and their dogs were horses.

Although life on the Montana prairie offered plenty of amusements, it also had its hazards. One of these was the buffalo, which could take life as well as sustain it. When Pretty Shield was seven, she had a chilling encounter with a mad bull that left her scarred for life. She was digging turnips with a sharp stick made from the branch of a chokecherry tree when the massive buffalo charged her, its face lathered with foam. She ran, but the string of one moccasin tangled in the sagebrush and sent her sprawling. The fall drove the digging stick into her forehead and up against one eye. It took three months for her to recover, and miraculously, she didn't lose her sight.

Grizzlies were also a menace, especially for women and children, whose job it was to pick the same kinds of berries the bears ate. Pretty Shield described one gory encounter that resulted in a woman's death. But not every confrontation with "those big, white bears" ended in tragedy. Pretty Shield recalled one incident that made everybody laugh—everybody, that is, except her and her companions.

It was July, and fourteen-year-old Pretty Shield and five other girls were away from the village digging turnips. As Pretty Shield stood to rest her aching back, she noticed horsemen approaching. Fearing that they were Sioux warriors, she and the other girls ran to a large pine tree and climbed into its branches to hide, their hearts "beating like war drums."

As the riders drew closer, Pretty Shield and her friends realized that they were Crow and that they were dragging something through the dust kicked up by their horses. The young men had roped a mother grizzly and two cubs. Pretty Shield described what happened next.

These young men were used to watching the country. They had seen us girls climb the tree, and now they rode straight to the pine, with their angry bears growling and scratching in every direction. "Come down, girls! Come down and play with our little pets!" they called, looking out for themselves all the time, keeping the bears from getting too near their horses.

When we wouldn't come down, and told them so, those young men tied their three bears to our tree, and then rode away, leaving them there. . . .

The day was so hot and still that not even a leaf stirred. . . . Always when I looked down, and I did this all the time, that old woman-bear was looking up at *me*. I saw that she was old, that her teeth were nearly all gone, and that her heavy claws were worn out; but her eyes were bad to look at. I was afraid. We girls scarcely spoke to each other, hardly moved. The limbs that we sat on began to hurt us, and yet we were afraid even to change our positions. . . .

I could *smell* those bears, and the smell made me sick. I was afraid of falling from the tree. The thought of falling down on that old-woman bear made me hang on to my limb until my fingers cramped.

Finally, when Pretty Shield was near tears, her father came to her rescue. He and two of the jokesters freed the mother bear and one of the cubs and gave the other to Pretty Shield's aunt, who "always kept a pet bear, because her medicine was the bear." Pretty Shield had fond memories of the roly-poly pet.

When my father gave my aunt this little cub she took it in her arms, and . . . the little bear wiggled its ears as though it felt happy. At first she carried it in her lap when we moved camp. Then when it grew bigger it rode on top of a pack, like a baby. But finally, like all the others, it got cross from being teased, and had to be sent away. But it used to follow the travois, after it grew too heavy to ride on a pack, as though it belonged to the Crow tribe, and I was sorry to see it go away.

When Pretty Shield was thirteen, her father promised her to a man named Goes Ahead, who would later serve as a scout for Lieutenant Colonel George Armstrong Custer at the Battle of the Little

Bighorn. At sixteen, Pretty Shield became Goes Ahead's second wife. Her oldest sister was his first, and her youngest sister eventually would become his third. Although Pretty Shield hardly knew Goes Ahead when they married, she learned to love him, she said, because he was always kind.

Among the Crows, the roles of men and women were strictly defined. As Pretty Shield explained, the men were responsible for hunting, stealing horses, and fighting Crow enemies. Women cared for their children, gathered wood, cooked and dried meat, tanned skins and dressed robes, and made clothes and lodges. When the tribe moved camp, it was the women who took down the lodges, packed the horses and travois, and put up the tepees in their new location.

Pretty Shield was the only wife of Goes Ahead to have children: three girls and two boys. She also lost a boy and a girl in infancy. It was in the course of grieving the latter death that she had a vision which led her to become a healer.

When a Crow woman was in mourning, she usually cut her hair short and slashed her arms, legs, and face to show her suffering. Then she wandered alone without food or water until her grief abated.

Pretty Shield had been in mourning for two months, sleeping little and eating only enough to stay alive, when she saw the apparition of a woman who led her to an anthill. Pretty Shield described the vision to Linderman.

> "Rake up the edges of this ant hill and ask for the things that you wish, daughter," the Person said; and then she was gone. Only the ant hill was there; and a wind was blowing. I saw the grass tremble as I was trembling, when I raked up the edges of the ant hill, as the Person had told me. Then I made my wish, "Give me good luck, and a

good life," I said aloud, looking at the hills. . . .

And even now the ants help me. I listen to them always. They are my medicine, these busy, powerful little people, the ants.

As a healer, Pretty Shield treated the physical ailments of Crow women and children and offered them spiritual counseling as well. She had a reputation for being an expert in the use of medicinal plants and was a much-respected member of the tribe. Like other Crow healers, she didn't charge for her services but received gifts of tobacco, elk teeth, food, and buffalo robes.

Pretty Shield lived a long life—long enough to witness the extermination of the buffalo and the subjugation of her people by the U.S. government. She watched the disappearance of Crow culture as it had existed for centuries. Pressed by Linderman, she sadly described this turning point in her people's history.

> The happiest days of my life were spent following the buffalo herds over our beautiful country. . . . There were always so many, many buffalo, plenty of good fat meat for everybody. . . .
>
> Ah, my heart fell down when I began to see dead buffalo scattered all over our beautiful country, killed and skinned, and left to rot by white men, many, many hundreds of buffalo. . . . The whole country there [the Judith Basin] smelled of rotting meat. Even the flowers could not put down the bad smell. Our hearts were like stone. . . .
>
> We believed for a long time that the buffalo would again come to us; but they did not. . . .

Times have changed so fast that they have left me behind. I do not understand these times. I am walking in the dark. Ours was a different world before the buffalo went away, and I belong to that other world.

Pretty Shield may have longed for the past, but her memories helped to preserve Crow heritage for later generations. Her tales and descriptions as transcribed by Linderman were pictures of her culture, powerful images that enabled Crow traditions to thrive in later days. ❧

MONTANA HISTORICAL SOCIETY, HELENA

Lucia Darling

LUCIA DARLING PARK

Pioneering Teacher

Lucia Darling stood on the crest of Salt Lake Hill and skeptically surveyed the valley below. For the past three months, she and the other members of her wagon train had jolted across mountains and plains, heading for a place they had come to think of as their "Valley of Promise." On September 18, 1863, they had finally reached their destination, and the scene before them, Lucia later wrote, "was not an inspiring one."

Below them on the banks of Grasshopper Creek sprawled the slapdash mining camp known as Bannack City—site of the first significant gold strike in what would one day be Montana. Lucia noted that there were "log houses of varying sizes and descriptions. In the distance, the most conspicuous sight was the gallows, fittingly erected near the graveyard in Hangman's Gulch, just beyond the town."

As Lucia and her companions stood speechless with disappointment at the looks of their new home, a four-year-old boy in their party voiced the thought that might well have crossed all their minds: "Say, Papa," he said, "I fink Bangup [Bannack] is a humbug."

Twenty-three-year-old Lucia had arrived at the barbarous boomtown with her uncle, Sidney Edgerton, and his family. Earlier that year, President Abraham Lincoln had appointed Edgerton chief justice of the newly created Idaho Territory, which then encompassed all of what is now Montana. So Lucia and the Edgertons had packed their belongings and left their home in Tallmadge, Ohio, to head west via train, riverboat, and covered wagon.

When they reached Bannack, the family settled in a five-room cabin that squatted on the bank of Grasshopper Creek, a tributary of the Beaverhead River. Although the log shack with its leaky sod roof and single small window suffered in comparison to the picket-fenced home they had left behind, Lucia considered it "very home-like and comfortable" once they had stretched carpets over the floor and hung pictures on the muslin-covered walls. As she explained with characteristic optimism, "[one] is not inclined to be fastidious as to the style of the house he occupies" after many months of hard travel.

Bannack in 1863 was a turbulent and lawless place, a jumble of saloons, gambling halls, and hurdy-gurdy houses bulging with high-spirited miners. The ready availability of gold—an estimated five million dollars' worth was taken from the gulch in the first year alone—had attracted a notorious band of outlaws led by none other than the charming and handsome local sheriff, Henry Plummer.

An early Bannack resident, Emily Meredith, offered a blunt assessment of the town in a letter she wrote to her father in April 1863:

> I don't know how many deaths have occurred this winter, but that there have not been twice as many is entirely owing to the fact that drunken men do not shoot well.

There are times when it is really unsafe to go through the main street on the other side of the creek, the bullets whizz around so, and no one thinks of punishing a man for shooting another. What do you think of a place where men will openly walk the street with shotguns, waiting to shoot some one against whom they have a grudge, and no one attempts to prevent it?

Granville Stuart, one of the first successful prospectors and cattlemen in Montana and later one of the state's most prominent citizens, had an equally dim view of the place. In his book *Forty Years on the Frontier*, he wrote:

The rich "diggings" of Grasshopper creek attracted many undesirable characters and I believe there were more desperadoes and lawless characters in Bannack in the winter of 1862-3 than ever infested any other mining camp of its size. Murders, robberies, and shooting scrapes were of frequent occurrence. . . . There was no safety for life or property only so far as each individual could, with his trusty rifle, protect his own.

Still, as Stuart acknowledged, the respectable folk far outnumbered the outlaws, and they were eager to bring a semblance of civilization to this infant settlement. When word got out that Lucia had been a teacher in Ohio, parents in Bannack begged her to open a school for their children. She consented.

Her first task was to find a suitable classroom. With her uncle as escort, she visited one of the town's most prominent landowners to ask if he could provide a place. Forty-one years later, in 1904, she still vividly remembered the encounter.

With some difficulty, we found his humble residence and rapped loudly at the door. For some time, no one responded, but finally a man's voice called "Come in." Pushing open the door, we saw in the dim light a man lying on buffalo robes on the floor. He did not rise to meet us, for he had not fully recovered from the results of imbibing too freely from the favorite and profuse beverage then so plentiful, and his voice was still too thick to be easily understood. My Uncle stated to him our errand. "Yes, glad of it," he said, "D——d shame, children running around the streets, ought to be in school. I will do anything I can to help her, she can have this room. . . . I will give it to her for cheap. She shall have it for fifty dollars a month. . . . It is dirt cheap."

Taking in the rude cabin with its mud-plastered walls, sod roof, and earthen floor, Lucia decided that, yes, the place offered plenty of dirt, but it was by no means cheap.

And so it was that she opened her school, often credited with being the first in Montana, in the front room of the Edgertons' own home—and in the shadow of the gallows that would soon see frequent use.

Lucia Aurora Darling was born October 9, 1839, near Kalamazoo, Michigan. Her mother died when she was ten, so she went to live with her relatives, the Edgertons, in Ohio. Well-educated, she began teaching public school there at the age of fourteen.

Although Lucia's early life was comfortable and sheltered, she had a lively, dauntless nature that stood her in good stead during her westward journey. Her courage and high spirits are evident in the daily record she kept of the slow and arduous trip to Idaho Territory.

The first part of the adventure was pleasant enough. Lucia and her relatives traveled by train to Saint Joseph, Missouri, and then by riverboat to Omaha. There, they spent a week buying covered wagons, oxen, guns, milk cows, ponies for the children to ride, and a dog they hoped would serve as both sentry and hunter. They also stocked up on provisions: bacon, ham, coffee, tea, salt, sugar, dried fruit, and canned peaches. The women bought silk masks designed to protect their complexions from the sun, wind, and rain. Finally, the party of sixteen, which included Lucia's cousin Wilbur Fisk Sanders and his family, squeezed their belongings into their wagons and pointed their oxen west.

Life on the Oregon Trail soon became fairly routine. The emigrants rose early and ate a hearty breakfast of coffee, ham or bacon, biscuits or pancakes, gravy, and milk. They stopped for an hour or two at midday and then halted early enough in the evening to get supper, milk the cows, put up a tent, and gather fuel for a fire before dark. To keep their spirits up, they often indulged in "a jolly time" of singing and telling stories in the moonlight or playing checkers over a meal. Lucia, in "calico dress and cordia sun bonnet," often wandered away from the train to explore the local landmarks. She also passed her time reading, napping, picking and pressing wildflowers, and writing frequent letters home.

Each day, the Edgertons' wagon train crept ten to twenty miles closer to Bannack, sometimes in a torrent of rain. Along the way, it passed hundreds of rotting buffalo carcasses, as well as several graves of unfortunate travelers. On July 3, Lucia described one of the latter.

> Passed a little grave by the roadside—the board at the head containing the name of Lora Hough. The sight was a sad one to us, for we have the long journey before us and nothing worse could happen to us than to have to leave one of our member in a lonely grave like this one.

The trip was always tiring, sometimes frightening, and often uncomfortable. Lucia bathed in muddy rivers and cold mountain streams, slept in a crowded wagon or on the hard ground beneath, and blistered her hands cooking over a small camp stove. She also took her turn at guard duty, watching in the night for Indians, bears, and hungry wolves with a loaded revolver by her side. As it turned out, the party had more trouble with mosquitos than with native peoples or wild animals.

Lucia and her family seemed to take most hardships of their journey in stride. Once, when one of the men returned empty-handed from a hunting foray, she described the party's reaction in her journal. "As we saw him coming we thought he had game on his shoulder which proved to be his boots," she wrote, "and which we demanded to fry for supper as he had brought nothing else."

Despite their unenthusiastic first impression of Bannack, Lucia and her fellow travelers must have been relieved to reach the end of their trail. But as Lucia soon discovered, life for the thirty or so family women in town was unusually confining. According to her cousin, Martha Edgerton Plassman,

> there was almost no visiting among the women. . . . Women stayed at home and generally found plenty to keep them occupied in the absence of conveniences. Marketing could have been regarded as amusement but marketing was not safe where pistol play was the chief amusement of some of the male inhabitants. . . .
>
> Shopping, it will be understood from this, partook of the nature of a foray into the enemy's country, and was not to be lightly considered. Among the earliest pioneers, men did most of the marketing and nearly all the gossiping.

So Lucia entertained herself by sewing, reading, and singing. If she did venture out of the house, it was usually to go riding or to pick berries—and, of course, to teach school.

Lucia's school opened in October 1863. At first, her dozen or so students attended class only in the morning. They had no desks and no standardized textbooks but used whatever they could scrape together. The room was heated by a temperamental wood stove, and classes were dismissed in mid-December because of extreme cold. They would resume again in the spring.

Meanwhile, however, Lucia's students were free to witness one of the most terrible chapters in the history of Montana. Fed up with the more than one hundred murders and robberies attributed to the Plummer gang, several men from the gold camps of Bannack, Virginia, and Nevada Cities—Wilbur Fisk Sanders prominent among them—met in secret two days before Christmas to form a "vigilance committee." Their intention was to take the law into their own hands and hurry the wheels of justice along.

In the next month, the Vigilantes, as they became known, executed twenty-two desperados, four of them in Bannack. On January 10, 1864, the bodies of Sheriff Plummer and two of his cohorts dangled from the gallows in Hangman's Gulch, within sight of Lucia's home and classroom. Another man, "Dutch John," joined them at the end of the rope two days later.

Although Lucia's school has commonly been referred to as the first in Montana, it by no means represented the first effort at schooling in the region. Catholic missionaries had taught Native American children as early as the 1840s, and a school was established in the fall of 1861 at Fort Owen in the Bitterroot Valley for children of the traders there. During the summer of 1863, Kate Dunlap taught in Nevada City, and Mrs. Henry Zoller taught primary students for two months in Bannack.

But Lucia may well be described as the first Montanan to teach a full term of school in a building erected solely for that purpose. At the beginning of her second year of classes, when her enrollment had swelled to twenty students and outgrown the Edgerton home, a pair of local men built a log schoolhouse on the opposite side of Grasshopper Creek. It later was used for committee meetings by the first territorial legislature.

As it happened, another member of Lucia's family also played a ground-breaking role in Montana education. Her uncle Sidney Edgerton—first governor of Montana Territory—convinced the legislature to create a public school system.

Lucia and the Edgertons didn't stay long in Montana. In 1865, they returned to Ohio, and shortly after the Civil War ended, Lucia went to Selma, Alabama, to teach emancipated black slaves. For nine years, she served as principal of the women's section of Berea College in Kentucky.

On September 17, 1885, Lucia married Servetus W. Park, a successful banker and businessman who had two children from a previous marriage. They settled in Warren, Ohio, where Lucia was a tireless church and civic worker. She was such an asset to her community that her death on August 18, 1905, was prominently reported on page one of the local newspaper. In it, she was described as "a woman of unusual intelligence combined with rare tact and a heart full of sympathy."

Although her time in Bannack was brief, Lucia Darling Park played an important role in the development of Montana. By bringing with her to the West the influence of education, she helped the territory mold its new citizens and fostered hope for its future. ❧

MATTIE CASTNER

Mother of Belt

For fourteen-year-old Mattie, the first day of 1863 was more than just the dawn of a new year. It would turn out to be the beginning of a whole new life. Of course, she probably didn't realize that as she clambered out of bed in the morning and groped for her clothes in the dark. She probably just went about her work as usual, caring for the children of her master, Robert Setzer. Since birth, her destiny had been in the hands of this North Carolina plantation owner. But that was about to change.

Many miles away, across the contested border between North and South, President Abraham Lincoln awoke knowing that this would be one of the most significant days in the history of his shattered nation. This was the day he would take gold pen in hand and sign the Emancipation Proclamation, delivering a fatal blow to what he considered "a moral, social, and political evil." The document declared that "on the 1st day of January, A.D. 1863, all persons held as slaves within any State or designated part of a State the people whereof shall then be in rebellion against the United States shall be then, thenceforward, and forever free."

COURTESY OF ETHEL M. KENNEDY

The Castner home and hotel in Belt.
John Castner is at the far right.

There is no record of Mattie's reaction to this momentous news. Perhaps her sentiments were similar to those of a Philadelphia black girl, whose soul, she recorded, was "glad with exceeding great gladness" on that "grand, glorious day."

Whatever Mattie may have thought at the time, the Emancipation Proclamation changed her life forever. For her, as for four million other black slaves, it opened the door to a new and potentially brighter future.

Mattie was born into slavery in Newton, North Carolina, on April 10, 1848. Sources differ on whether her maiden name was Bost, Bell, or some combination of the two.

President Lincoln had once referred to the West as the place "for poor people to go to and better their condition." Mattie, too, began to view the frontier as the land of opportunity. After slavery was abolished, Mattie moved to Saint Louis, Missouri, where she found work as a housekeeper, nanny, and hotel maid. By 1876, she was caring for the two children of the Sire family. When Mrs. Sire moved to Fort Benton, Montana Territory, Mattie agreed to stay behind with the children until their mother was settled. Then, in the spring of 1876, Mattie and her charges boarded the steamboat *Nellie Peck* and made the long journey to Montana to join her employer.

Soon after her arrival in Fort Benton in June, Mattie took a job as a laundress at the Overland Hotel, earning one hundred dollars a month, a large sum in those days. Sometime later, she opened her own laundry. It was there that she met John K. Castner, a hardworking, white Pennsylvania man who hauled freight by mule between Fort Benton and Helena. In 1877, the pair traveled to Helena, the territorial capital, to be married.

Seven years earlier, Castner had explored the region around Fort Benton and had discovered coal formations in a valley thirty-five miles to the southwest. In 1877, he had filed mining claims and, with a partner, had begun digging the coal and hauling it to Fort Benton. He sold it for four dollars a ton, to local residents and to operators of the steamboats plying the Missouri River.

Now, he and his bride Mattie moved to the valley and built a log cabin beside a winding creek. They covered it with brush, cemented it with mud and buffalo chips, and lined it with unbleached muslin painted with a whitewash of zinc oxide, water, and glue. This modest home was to become the nucleus of the town of Belt, Montana.

It wasn't long before the Castner cabin grew into the Castner Hotel, a stopping place for travelers taking the stagecoach between the towns of Great Falls and Lewistown. As traffic on the road increased, the Castners built additions to their log home until it became a sprawling, mazelike structure. Sometimes, people even got lost in its meandering hallways.

Mattie managed the hotel and prepared all the meals served in its dining room. She soon became "famous among cowboys, stockmen, sheepherders, lawyers, preachers, gamblers, and politicians" for her culinary talent. She served an abundance of wild game, including grouse, prairie chickens, deer, antelope, elk, buffalo, and trout. Much of it she brought home from her own hunting and fishing expeditions. She cooked vegetables from her garden, and "her creamed peas were the best in the world," according to her granddaughter, Ethel Castner Kennedy. These savory meals cost fifty cents apiece and attracted diners from many miles away.

Ethel Kennedy, who ate at the Castner Hotel as a small child in the early 1900s, remembered her grandmother as a short woman who always wore a maroon sweater and kept a parrot. Sometimes these birds would develop a naughty vocabulary, no doubt under the tutelage of bawdy guests. Once the birds had been so corrupted, Mattie would banish them from her home and quickly find replacements.

Mattie was well-received by the people of Montana Territory, despite the recent war that had split the nation over the issue of slavery. According to *Belt Valley History*, "Mattie commanded the respect of the people in Belt because of her generosity, industry, and integrity, and probably, to some extent, because she was the wife of John K. Castner, the highly regarded founder of Belt."

Mattie Castner was an astute and ambitious woman. In addition to running the hotel, she was sometimes seen swinging a pick at her husband's coal mines. Three times a week in early summer, she would ride to Fort Benton to sell homegrown produce. She would load her vegetables into a wagon after sundown and, after driving all night, reach her destination about dawn.

As the Castners found success, Mattie began to buy land, including a 640-acre ranch in the Highwood Mountains. By the time of her death, she was the largest individual property owner in Belt. Meanwhile, her husband John pursued his own commercial interests. In addition to mining, he became involved in mercantiles, real estate, and insurance. When the town of Belt was incorporated in 1907, Castner was unanimously selected to be its first mayor. For several years, he was chairman of the town's board of education.

Despite having grown up with little to call her own, Mattie was generous with her newfound prosperity and donated often to civic causes. Her granddaughter recalled that Mattie would prepare baskets of food for needy townspeople and deliver them after dark. She wanted to spare the poor people the shame of having to accept charity, Ethel Kennedy explained.

Mattie's generosity showed itself in another, more personal way. Although she never had children of her own, she raised a baby boy abandoned at the hotel in about 1880. The Castners named the lad Albert and called him their own. He had been the first white child born in Belt—on December 18, 1879—and he lived there most of his life, maintaining a close relationship with his foster parents.

Mattie tried to renew other family ties as well. She made three trips back to North Carolina, hoping to find her parents and five brothers and sisters. Various sources say she located a niece, a brother, and two sisters. Some of her relatives returned with her to Montana, where she gave them jobs at her hotel. The others had been sold when Mattie was young, and no one knew their whereabouts.

Mattie retired from the hotel business around 1912. Three years later, she found her husband dead in his bed, the victim of heart disease. Mattie died of "dropsy," or edema, on April 2, 1920, in the midst of a record-breaking blizzard. She left an estate of $25,000—a substantial sum. Characteristically, she donated most of it to charity.

In 1989, Mattie Castner was added to the Gallery of Outstanding Montanans in the state Capitol. As the plaque hung in her honor so aptly says,

> Montana lost more than a leading citizen with Mattie's death; it lost the sense of community spirit that "the Mother of Belt" personified. Mattie Castner's career in Montana epitomizes the "pioneer spirit" on which the state has been built in the twentieth century. ❧

Helen P. Clarke

Indian Advocate

$\mathcal{M}$alcolm Clarke and his twenty-four-year-old daughter, Helen, were engrossed in a game of backgammon when they heard their dogs announce a visitor. They glanced up, startled. Who would call at their ranch north of Helena, Montana Territory, at nine o'clock in the evening? It must be a Blackfeet Indian, the pair decided. The neighboring Blackfeet, unfettered by the customs of white society, sometimes knocked on the Clarkes' door in the middle of the night.

Father and daughter returned their attention to the game. The arrival of Blackfeet didn't worry them. After all, Malcolm's wife Coth-co-co-na was a Pikuni Blackfeet herself; one of her relatives had probably come to call. But the sounds of hurrying feet and strange voices finally broke Helen's concentration. She put down her dice and bustled to the back of the house to find out who was there.

In the kitchen, Helen's mother and two sisters were greeting a handful of Blackfeet braves, including Ne-tus-che-o, Coth-co-co-na's cousin. The smiling warrior pumped Malcolm's hand and embraced Helen's twenty-year-old brother, Horace. Malcolm showed

Helen P. Clarke

MONTANA HISTORICAL SOCIETY, HELENA

his hospitality by filling his pipe and passing it to one of the visitors. The men sat in a circle, puffing in turn, while Coth-co-co-na and her aunt, Black Bear, prepared a meal for them.

The Clarkes had no reason to fear their Blackfeet kin, even though relations between the tribe and white settlers had soured in the past month. The trouble had started earlier that summer of 1869 when some residents of Fort Benton had murdered two Blackfeet—an old man and a boy—in retaliation for the deaths of two white cattle herders who, it turned out, had been killed by Crows. The incident had spawned a rash of horse thefts and murderous attacks on isolated ranches.

Two years earlier, some of Ne-tus-che-o's horses had been stolen by white men while he was a guest at the Clarke ranch. Horses were among the most prized possessions of the nomadic Blackfeet, and the outraged warrior responded by abducting some of the Clarkes' herd. When Malcolm and Horace went to the Blackfeet village to retrieve their animals, they found Ne-tus-che-o seated on the younger Clarke's favorite mount. Horace lost his temper, called the warrior a dog, and lashed him across the face with his riding whip. Fortunately, Malcolm and some of the tribal elders intervened and kept the confrontation from ending in bloodshed.

Certainly Ne-tus-che-o's behavior on this balmy August evening implied that he'd put the quarrel behind him. In fact, the Blackfeet announced that they had come to return some horses taken from the Clarkes three years earlier by members of a Canadian tribe of Blackfeet, the Bloods. They also wanted to tell Malcolm—or Four Bears, as they called him—that he was welcome to come and trade with their village.

As Horace prepared to go identify the horses the visitors had brought with them, Helen noticed that the warriors seemed agitated. One of them paced the room, fingering the family's belongings. But the behavior didn't trouble her. When Horace couldn't find his gun belt to take with him, she told him "What is the use of a firearm? You are with a friend." Horace left the house unarmed in the company of one of the Blackfeet men.

Meanwhile, Malcolm and the others continued to chat. Helen noticed that Ne-tus-che-o kept his hands hidden in his blanket, and she wondered briefly if he were cold. Then he and her father rose to go outside for a private conversation. The door had scarcely closed behind them when a gunshot cracked the peace. Helen later described the pandemonium that followed.

> I was seized with a sudden faintness. . . . I went to [the door]; and imagine my terror at the confusion that passed before my vision. Horses and Indians running backwards and forwards with aimless purpose. Not one, not two, but hundreds it seemed to me, and for a moment I thought the demons in hell had broken loose. . . .
>
> Just then I heard my brother's voice. He was about a hundred yards away. Clear and distinct his words fell on my ears: "Father, I am shot." [But] father had already received his final blow. The shot that was fired at the moment Horace's words came to me was the fatal one. . . . [M]y heart's premonitions had already told me that he had passed into the shadowy river, and was far on his way into the unknown land. I ran out to assist Horace; even then I could not, would not, believe it was Blackfeet who had done this deed. . . . I said to Horace: "It was not that Indian who went with you that shot you . . . ! It was a Pend d'Oreille, was it not?" "No, Nellie, it was that one," he replied. . . . It was so hard to believe that they, the

Pi-kan-ies, our blood, had proved so unworthy of the trust we had reposed in them.

Horace had been shot in the face and left for dead. Although he was bleeding heavily, he had managed to crawl close enough to the house to call for help. Along with her great aunt, Black Bear, Helen lugged him inside and laid him in a rude bed she made on the floor of her father's room. He was faint with the loss of blood, and she wondered how she could ever staunch the flow. Then she thought of an old Blackfeet remedy. Frantically, she grabbed her father's tobacco pouch, wet the contents, and applied them to Horace's gaping wound.

Meanwhile, Helen's eleven-year-old sister, Isabel, had discovered their father. He lay within a few feet of the house with a bullet through his heart and the gash of an ax across his brow. Helen, her mother, and Black Bear managed to haul him into the house and lay him in the middle of the main room. Then, Black Bear went looking for the attackers, to try to talk them out of more bloody vengeance.

Helen knew the Blackfeet warriors would likely be back. The front door had no lock, so Coth-co-co-na dragged a heavy bedstead in front of it. As she passed a window, a bullet whizzed by her head. The family decided to barricade itself in Helen's room, which was toward the back of the house. Though they knew it was pointless, they nailed the door shut. Then they huddled together, listening for sounds of the men's return. For an hour, all was quiet.

Finally, the terrorized family heard the tramping of horses. Through the bedroom door, they could hear the intruders enter the house and begin ransacking the family's belongings. They cringed at the sounds of shattering glass and splintering wood. Then came the most frightening sounds of all. The familiar Blackfeet voices began to argue over what to do with the family. Helen later recalled their horrifying debate.

> We kept so still—so still. Death seemed awaiting us. One or two of them were in favor of taking us prisoners; others in favor of killing us. My mother was to die any way. Ne-tus-che-o then said: "Horace is alive, he is somewhere in the house, and he is in that room," pointing to mine. He had his hand on the door, about to enter. The door creaked and groaned. My brother, weak as he was, rose to his feet with hatchet raised, determined to make a resolute struggle for his mother and his sisters.

But fate—in the form of Helen's great aunt, Black Bear—intervened just in time. The old woman tried to reason with the warriors, claiming that Horace was dead and begging them to take pity. "The man murdered to-night was your best friend," she scolded. "You have committed a deed so dark, so terrible that the trees will whisper it, and before the sun reddens these mountains a hundred horsemen will be here to avenge his death."

The Blackfeet braves faltered. "That which the old woman utters is true," Helen heard one of them say. "Enough blood has been shed. I came not here to make war on women and children."

It was about midnight when the warriors galloped away, driving the Clarkes' cattle before them and venting their rage and frustration by shooting into the herd. The family huddled in the dark until five in the morning, when a hint of daylight revealed no one lurking in the yard. Helen and Isabel hiked three-quarters of a mile to the nearest ranch for help, all the while fearing the warriors would leap at them from the underbrush like hungry wolves. But they made it safely.

That afternoon, a doctor arrived from Helena, twenty-five miles south, and was able to give them encouraging news. Horace would recover fully from his wound. Two days later, on August 19, 1869, the Clarkes buried their patriarch—one of the most prominent men in the region—at the mouth of Little Prickly Pear Canyon.

Unfortunately, the clash between whites and Blackfeet didn't end with Clarke's tragic murder. In response to settlers' demands for reprisal, Major Eugene M. Baker set out from Fort Ellis in January 1870 with orders to find Ne-tus-che-o's band and "strike them hard." On a bitter cold morning, he and his troops attacked an unsuspecting Blackfeet village and slaughtered 173 of its occupants, including fifty-three women and children. But it was the wrong village. This was not Ne-tus-che-o's band. It was that of a peaceable Blackfeet chief. Easterners were outraged, but the Baker Massacre, as the incident became known, largely ended Blackfeet resistance to white invasion of their homeland.

The murder of Malcolm Clarke had a lasting effect on Helen's life. Soon after, she was sent to live with an aunt in Cincinnati, Ohio, but she didn't succumb to bitterness and reject her mother's people. She wisely realized that Malcolm's murder was the act of a few vengeful individuals, not the desire of the Blackfeet nation. Twenty years later, she would return to Montana to help the tribe adjust to the new ways of life imposed on them by the U.S. government.

Helen Clarke was born on October 11 at a fur-trading post at the mouth of the Judith River in what would one day be Fergus County, Montana. In those days, no one bothered to record the birth of a child in the wilderness, so the year in which Helen was born is uncertain. Her death certificate, for which her sister Isabel supplied much of the information, puts it at 1845. Her obituary says 1848, and her tombstone says 1846.

Helen's father, Egbert Malcolm Clarke, was a graduate of West

Point, who came to the Northern Rockies in 1841 to work as a clerk for the American Fur Company. A few years later, he married Coth-co-co-na, the daughter of a Pikuni chief. Helen—or Nellie, as her friends and family called her—was the oldest of the couple's four children. Her Blackfeet name, Pio-to-po-waka, has been translated as Bird That Comes Home.

At the age of three, Helen went to live with an aunt in Minneapolis, Minnesota, and attended convent schools there. She returned to Montana to live with her parents sometime in the 1860s, when Malcolm left the fur-trading business and established a horse and cattle ranch on Prickly Pear Creek. After his tragic death, she went back East again, this time to live with another aunt in Cincinnati. She continued her education there and went on to attend a school of drama in New York City.

Helen's striking appearance and deep, vibrant voice helped to launch a brief but impressive theatrical career. She performed in New York, London, Paris, and Berlin, at least once sharing the stage with the famous French actress Sarah Bernhardt. The German Kaiser once commended her portrayal of Shakespeare's Lady Macbeth.

But Helen soon grew disillusioned with acting and was unconvinced of her talent. "I was too much . . . [my]self to become great," she once wrote. "I could not forget that I was Helen Clarke and become the new being of imagination."

So in 1875, Helen returned to Montana and taught school in Fort Benton and Helena. Seven years later, she was elected Lewis and Clark County superintendent of schools, apparently making her the first woman ever to hold elective office in Montana.

Helen never married, although she had plenty of suitors. According to some accounts, she didn't think she could find a man who would neither pity nor patronize her for having mixed blood, and she didn't want a relationship in which she was not an equal.

Yet she never denied her heritage. Once, in fact, she made a point of responding to a newspaper article that claimed she was ashamed of her Blackfeet blood. Indignant, she told *The Montana Daily Record* in Helena,

> Now, as a matter of fact, I am far from being ashamed of my origin, but, on the other hand am proud of both my father and mother. My father was one of the first settlers of the Northwest. . . . He was one of the old-timers of Fort Benton, and, like many pioneers, married an Indian girl. She was a good woman, a good wife and a loving mother, and why anyone should be ashamed of her is more than I can comprehend.

Helen got a chance to serve her mother's people in 1891, when the federal Office of Indian Affairs asked her to act as an interpreter and mediator on the Blackfeet reservation in northern Montana. Her job was to help the Blackfeet understand and accept a new law that required each family to choose a plot of land on which to settle and farm. Officials wanted Native Americans to assimilate into white culture, and the Interior Department considered land allotments the best solution to the problem of "civilizing" these native people.

Helen was one of only a few women to help manage the federal allotment program. Because of her success on the Blackfeet reservation, she was transferred to Oklahoma to work with the Ponca, Oto, Pawnee, and Missouri tribes. She returned to Montana in 1895 to help the Blackfeet negotiate the sale of the mountainous western section of their reservation, which would become part of Glacier National Park.

In 1900 Helen moved to San Francisco, where she taught public-speaking classes and took French lessons. But the glamour of city life soon paled, and in 1902, she applied for and got permission to live on the Blackfeet reservation and become an official member of the tribe. She went to live with her brother Horace on a cattle ranch near Midvale (now East Glacier), where she kept a large library and entertained writers, artists, and musicians from across the nation. Her door was always open to those who needed her help.

Helen died of pneumonia on March 5, 1923, and is buried in the shadow of the spectacular, snow-capped peaks of Glacier National Park. At her burial, a Catholic priest expressed the love and respect with which she would be remembered.

> Her life was an open book and on its every golden page are inscribed the good deeds of one who loved her God, her Church, her people, her country and was faithful to them. . . . She led a life of unbending integrity, a life of simple virtue, a life of unsullied honor. She ever carried with her a smiling cheerfulness, an unswerving devotion, a gentle courtesy. To those whose privilege it was to know her intimately, she was the friend the soul is ever seeking, the friend that understands, the friend that sympathizes, the friend that knows our weakness and still loves us, the friend that sees only the best in us. ✤

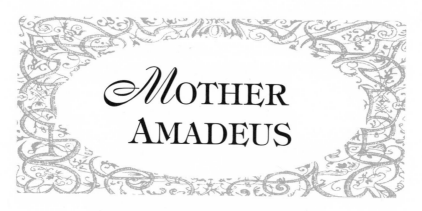

MOTHER AMADEUS

Lady Black Robe

On January 18, 1884, a train rattled into the station at Miles City, Montana Territory, and coasted to a stop with a great, steamy sigh. In a billow of black, six travel-weary nuns stepped down to the platform. There to greet them was a crowd made up mostly of crude and crusty cowboys.

In the 1880s, Miles City was a rowdy cow town with about 2,500 residents, two general stores, and sixty-five saloons. To its townspeople, the newly arrived representatives of God were a welcome—and morally uplifting—addition. According to one account, "the motley gathering . . . hailed the nuns with delirious enthusiasm, and those gathered about the saloons doffed their sombreros, removed their pipes, and observed a reverential silence when the nuns, with lowered veils, walked past."

The leader of this little flock of Ursuline nuns was Mother Mary Amadeus, a tireless and selfless woman who, even as a small child, had yearned to be a missionary among the Indians. In 1884, her ambition was about to be realized. Over the next three decades, despite chronic illness and crippling injury, she would open eight

MONTANA HISTORICAL SOCIETY, HELENA

Mother Amadeus

mission schools among the Native American tribes of Montana and three among the Eskimos of Alaska. The Cheyennes would call her Maka-mahe-hona-wihona, or The Great Holy White Chief Woman. The Eskimos would simply call her Anyachak, "Mother," and her name would become synonymous with Catholic missionary efforts in the West.

But on that frosty day in Miles City, Mother Amadeus had more pressing concerns than the salvation of souls. No one had thought to arrange a place for the nuns to stay. At the suggestion of Bishop John Brondel, who had come all the way from Helena, Montana, to welcome them, Mother Amadeus and her companions settled for the night at a boarding house owned by a widow named Bridget McCanna.

That first night must have been a true test of the Ursulines' faith. Their room was cold and filthy—so filthy they didn't dare use the single bed. They sat huddled all night on the floor, leaning against the thin wall that separated their quarters from a Chinese laundry. Snow and moonlight filtered through cracks in the walls and roof, and somewhere nearby they could hear a noisy craps game in progress.

The morning proved no more hospitable. According to Mother Amadeus's friend and biographer, Mother Angela Lincoln,

> as soon as the first streaks of dawn peopled the streets, the nuns left the house, and began the first of their many trails through the deep snow to the church. The night had turned it into a very block of ice. They unlocked it, and with hands frozen and unused to such labor, they gathered chips and made a big blazing fire. When the Bishop [Brondel] appeared in the sanctuary at 8 A.M., he was greeted by a genial warmth, the symbol of all his future dealings with Mother Amadeus and the Ursulines.

Later that day, Mother Amadeus set out to find a suitable house for a convent. She rented a small cottage on Palmer Street for about thirty dollars a month, paying for the first two months with money donated by a generous patron back home. She knew she would have to trust in Divine Providence to supply the rent in future months, because the nuns had no regular source of income.

Next, the nuns went shopping for provisions: a sack of flour, a dozen eggs, three pounds of tea, five pounds of coffee, a quart of milk, sixteen pounds of potatoes, three pounds of bologna, and six pounds of other meat. Mother Amadeus also bought a wood stove to heat their new home. That night, they slept on the floor wrapped in buffalo robes, their heads resting on whatever might pass for a pillow—a satchel, a Webster's dictionary, and, in Mother Amadeus's case, a world atlas.

Though they now had a better roof over their heads, the nuns had little else to call their own. The people of Miles City apparently hadn't considered how to provide for their welfare. In *Life of The Reverend Mother Amadeus*, Mother Angela described their meager daily existence and their serene acceptance of it.

> Now began for Mother Amadeus and her nuns the poetry of privation.... [L]ack of money made them suffer keenly for want of the simplest necessities.... [T]heir beds were. . . hard, and they were undoubtedly very hungry when they sat down to the scantily furnished table, their rations, short rations of corn meal and a half dozen oranges which a dealer brought because "They were rotten. I cannot sell them. . . ." And the nuns only laughed at the table and passed the bread plate about saying: "I'm not hungry."

One day, so the story goes, the chaplain from nearby Fort Keogh met a young girl running breathlessly down the street and stopped her to ask her errand. She was going, she said, to the butcher shop to buy ten cents' worth of liver for the nuns, and she hurried on. Horrified, the pastor devoted his next Sunday sermon to the bitter plight of the Ursulines. The abashed townspeople made sure the missionaries had plenty to eat after that.

Not long after their arrival in Montana, the nuns opened a boarding school in Miles City. Then, on March 30, 1884, Mother Amadeus and three of the Ursuline sisters set out for the Cheyenne Indian reservation to establish their first mission among the native people. With an escort of soldiers from Fort Keogh, they traveled southwest for four days across cactus-covered badlands, fording the Tongue River twice. At about noon on April 2, they reached their new home—an abandoned, three-room log cabin with a floor and roof of mud. It would be called Saint Labre's Mission, the first in a long line of charitable ventures founded by Mother Amadeus.

Mother Amadeus was born Sarah Theresa Dunne on July 2, 1846, in Akron, Ohio. She was the fifth child of Irish immigrants John and Ellen Dunne. When Sarah was small, her father and older brother joined the stampede to California to look for gold. In 1856, the rest of the family followed—except for Sarah and a sister, Mary, who were left at an Ursuline boarding school in Cleveland.

From the beginning, the Ursulines were favorably impressed with little Sarah. In the sentimental view of Mother Angela, she was

so tiny, so delicate, she stood in the sunshine of everyone's heart. . . . laughing, leading, praying, playing. Her brothers write of her: "She was our youngest, always considered pretty, very bright and active, good-natured, keen, witty, courageous. Her eyes were steel blue and very clear;

her hair, golden at age six, changed at nine to light brown; her forehead, rounded and protruding." The lines of the child's face mirrored her character—there were no angles—all was winning, sweet, attractive, sunny.

Mary Warner, Sarah's friend for sixty years, also recalled her in glowing terms.

Never was she rude or rough in look, word, or act.... In school, no one could surpass Sarah in class standing, so bright was she. Sarah would divest herself of everything to give pleasure to another. I never knew her to make an unkind remark of any human being, and this feature alone would mark her as one of God's darlings. Self-sacrifice was the leaven of her life.

Sarah showed an interest in the religious life even as a child. According to Mother Angela, she would sometimes tell her playmates, "Someday I shall be a missionary in the Rocky Mountains and in Alaska." When her parents summoned her and her sister to join them in California, Sarah refused, mincing no words. "We have the right to frame our own future," she wrote to them. "But if you insist, we shall both come, and if our lives prove unhappy, the blame will be on you." Needless to say, they relented.

After five years at the Cleveland boarding school, Sarah entered the Ursuline convent in Toledo, Ohio. There, on August 23, 1864, she pronounced her holy vows as Sister Mary Amadeus. Ten years later, when she was only twenty-eight, she was unanimously elected Mother Superior, head of the entire convent.

Meanwhile, Native Americans in Montana Territory were becoming increasingly bitter as white settlers swarmed onto their homelands and hunting grounds. Hostilities reached a climax on a hot, summer day in 1876, when several thousand Sioux and Cheyenne warriors annihilated Lieutenant Colonel George Armstrong Custer and his command at the Battle of the Little Bighorn. But their victory was short-lived. U.S. troops soon subdued the tribes and drove them onto reservations, forcing them to accept an uneasy truce.

Catholic authorities in Montana thought the presence of nuns among the vanquished peoples might help keep the peace. So, in 1881, an appeal went out for volunteers. When the news reached the Toledo convent where Mother Amadeus lived, thirty Ursulines offered to go West. Their bishop chose six of them and put Mother Amadeus, whom he considered the "flower of the flock," in charge. They set out for Montana in 1884.

For the next twenty-five years, Mother Amadeus and her nuns—known as "Lady Black Robes" since they were religious sisters to the black-robed Jesuit priests—traveled across Montana, establishing mission schools. Six months after opening Saint Labre's, she was called to Saint Peter's Mission, about thirty-five miles southwest of Great Falls, to found a boarding school for Indian girls. Then, in quick succession, came schools for the Gros Ventres and Assiniboines at Saint Paul's Mission on the Fort Belknap reservation (1887); for the Crows at Saint Francis Xavier on the Little Bighorn River (1887); for the Kalispels, Pend d'Oreilles, Kootenais, and Flatheads at Saint Ignatius in the Flathead Valley (1890); for the Blackfeet at Holy Family near Browning (1890); for Chief Plenty Coups and his Crow followers at Saint Charles in Pryor (1892); and for Chief Charlot and his Flathead people at Saint John Berchman in Arlee (1892). Mother Amadeus also founded two parochial academies in Anaconda.

Life at these missions was often harsh and grueling. In her book *Ursulines of the West*, Mother Clotilde McBride described some of the hardships that Mother Amadeus and her fellow nuns endured.

> Most of the experiences of those days were recorded only by guardian angels—the rigors of the weather and extreme poverty, snow up to the waists of the nuns, winds that blew them flat on the ground, their shoes often frozen to the floor when they tried to put them on in the morning, nights spent sitting up when the scanty supply of bed clothing had to be given to the children, sickness among members of the [Ursuline] community, malignant diseases among the children, time after time provisions running low until there was but a little oil and a handful of meal in the house.

The annals of the Ursulines are peppered with references to illness and death among the students and nuns and to fires on the prairie and at Saint Peter's Mission. One entry, on January 31, 1893, notes that the temperature one winter day in Helena was fifty-two degrees below zero, and another describes snowdrifts fourteen feet deep.

As if these trials weren't enough, Mother Amadeus often suffered bouts of nausea and vomiting, the results of an accidental poisoning when she was twenty-eight. Her diet consisted of little more than milk and bread. Because she was so frail, she also was a frequent victim of pneumonia. Very soon after her arrival at Saint Peter's, she became so ill that a priest administered the last rites. Remarkably, she recovered.

Mother Amadeus lived primarily at Saint Peter's Mission while in Montana and established a novitiate there, but she traveled extensively to oversee the Ursulines' other mission schools. These journeys through near-empty wilderness, across rugged mountains and bridgeless rivers, sometimes led to near disaster.

One such journey, in December 1894, almost ended in drowning. On her way to Billings from the Pryor school, Mother Amadeus and her companions had to ford Blue Creek, a tributary of the Yellowstone River. Her driver guided his wagon into the swollen stream but mistook the location of the ford. Mother Clotilde described what happened next.

> [The horses] halted abruptly, snorting and trembling. Icy water rose over the wheels and up to the waist of the nuns, while huge cakes of ice knocked against the carriage, threatening to overturn it at any moment. The driver fainted, but an Invisible Power held the horses. Mother Amadeus succeeded in rousing the man and then instructed him to crawl out carefully over the back wheels, get to shore, and go for help to a cowboy camp that they had passed on the way. For three quarters of an hour, the nuns sat motionless in that deathly water until aid came. . . . It was discovered the next day that the fore feet of the horses had stopped on the brink of a deep hole and that the hind legs of the poor animals had been floating in the stream.

On another occasion, while traveling from Saint Labre's to Saint Xavier's, Mother Amadeus's driver lost control of his horses. Seeing that they were headed toward a precipice, the nun warned her companions to jump—just before their buggy sailed over the edge of the cliff and was dashed to pieces below. As the party continued on foot, a pack of "gray and ghastly" wolves dogged their tracks. Mother Amadeus knelt and prayed, and the wolves disappeared as silently as they had come.

The famous and beloved nun was not so lucky in October 1902. On the way to Miles City by train, she was crippled for life when her eastbound locomotive crashed at full speed into a westbound train. She was thrown violently to the floor, breaking her hip. For nine weeks, she lay immobilized in a Helena hospital with heavy weights suspended from her feet. Yet, according to Mother Angela, she had "a smile, a word of counsel and consolation for every one." The badly set bones never healed properly, and Mother Amadeus carried a cane for the rest of her life. But even that couldn't stop her from exploring new frontiers.

Mother Amadeus traveled to Rome several times on business, and during one trip she got permission to found missions among the Eskimos of Alaska, fulfilling another lifelong dream. In 1905, she sent three nuns to Akulurak, a little village about ten miles from the Bering Sea, where they opened a mission known as Saint Mary's. She followed them to Alaska herself a few years later and spent the last years of her life shuttling back and forth between Alaska and a convent she had established in Seattle, Washington.

But Montana had not seen the last of Mother Amadeus. After her death in Seattle on November 10, 1919, she was brought back to Saint Ignatius and buried in the shadow of the Mission Mountains. At her graveside, the Flathead Indians chanted their traditional dirge for a fallen hero.

Mother Amadeus's magnanimous nature and magnetic personality inspired effusive tributes. Her friend and biographer Mother Angela saw in her something of a saint, noting that

> she had many bitter trials, she met with many heavy crosses, but she lifted and carried them. She led a life of incessant activity, walking painfully with a cane and

counting one sleepless night after another. . . . She was an organizer, a pioneer, and she has stamped her name upon the soil of Montana and Alaska. . . . Her unanswering, bouyant trust [in God] was catching and peculiarly characteristic. Yet she was as active, intelligent, and prudent, as untiring in her work as though its success depended entirely on herself and upon herself alone. . . . She had a mother's heart, and a mother's heart is the most perfect thing God has ever made.

Mother Amadeus and the Ursuline Sisters were not the only religious women to play a part in the development of Montana. Representatives of other Catholic orders, especially the Sisters of Charity of Leavenworth and the Sisters of Providence, braved primitive conditions and dire poverty to found schools and hospitals in the wilderness. Their influence can still be felt throughout the state in such communities as Helena, Great Falls, Missoula, Billings, and Butte—cities that have thrived in part because of their good works. ❧

MARY FIELDS

The White Crow

*M*other Mary Amadeus lay near death on the floor of her rough-hewn log cabin. For the past year, the Catholic nun and missionary had devoted her life to caring for Native American children in territorial Montana. Suffering from pneumonia on an April day in 1885, she needed a guardian angel of her own. She found one in the unlikely form of Mary Fields, a six-foot, two-hundred-pound former slave with a face "as black as a burnt-over prairie" and a penchant for fat cigars.

Mary Fields was born in Tennessee in 1832 and was freed with the signing of the Emancipation Proclamation more than thirty years later. She apparently met Mother Amadeus while working as a servant in the home of Judge Edmund Dunne, the nun's oldest brother. When the judge's wife died, Mary took the family's five children to stay with their aunt, who was by that time running the Ursuline convent in Toledo, Ohio. The sturdy domestic aide and the delicate nun soon became loyal friends.

In 1884, Bishop John Brondel, the first Catholic bishop of Montana, asked Mother Amadeus to come to Saint Peter's Mission,

MONTANA HISTORICAL SOCIETY, HELENA

Mary Fields

about thirty-five miles southwest of Great Falls, Montana Territory. He wanted her to establish a school for Native American girls and to oversee the education of the Blackfeet boys already there. Mary still worked at the Ohio convent, but when news of Mother Amadeus's illness reached Toledo, she knew where her allegiance lay. She hurried to Montana to nurse her ailing friend.

Miraculously, Mother Amadeus recovered her health, and Mary decided to remain at the mission to help in whatever way she could. For the next decade, she busied herself hauling freight, doing laundry, keeping a vegetable garden, and tending as many as four hundred chickens at a time.

Father Eli Lindesmith, an Army chaplain stationed at Fort Keogh near Miles City, Montana Territory, got an amusing glimpse of Mary's sense of duty when he visited Saint Peter's Mission in 1887. One morning, Mary discovered that a skunk had invaded the chicken coop and killed sixty-two of the baby chicks in her care. Father Lindesmith recorded her reaction in his diary:

> Mary was horrified but did not retreat but at once took a hoe and made fight on the skunk and killed the beast. And as positive proof that she killed the animal, Mary . . . picked up the [pole] cat by a leg and carried it to the convent a distance of about a mile, and there with a mingled spirit of indignation and triumph she made an eloquent description of the killing of the chickens by the cat and the fight and slaughter of the monster beast by herself, holding up and turning around and showing the skunk as an ocular demonstration of all she said and of all that had happened.
>
> I asked her the following question, "And Mary did not the pole cat throw his stench all over you?" Her an-

swer was "Oh, no Father. I attacked and killed him from the front, not the rear."

According to Father Lindesmith, Mary was "always in a good humor showing her pearly teeth in smiles." The Indians of the region, he said, called her the White Crow, "because she acts like a white woman but has a black skin."

Townsfolk weren't sure at first what to think of this big, black bear of a woman. Although Mary was in her fifties when she came to Montana, she soon earned a reputation for being as tough and fearless as any man. With a cigar clamped in her teeth, a pistol strapped under her apron, and a jug of whiskey by her side, she wasn't quite respectable in the opinion of some people. One schoolgirl made Mary the subject of an essay, commenting that the woman "drinks whiskey, and she swears, and she is a republican, which makes her a low, foul creature."

The Ursulines were more charitable in their assessment. In her book about Saint Peter's Mission, Sister Genevieve McBride conceded that Mary "was at times troublesome, but her unfailing loyalty endeared her to the Nuns and children." The *Cascade Echo* later noted in Mary's obituary that

> it was her chief delight to make glad and merry the hearts of the little folks, and while at the Mission it was her wont to take the children out on the hills there to view the beauty of God's handiwork; and enjoy themselves to the utmost and rest assured that Mary never failed to have secreted about her person the necessary lunch to make every picnic complete.

Nonetheless, Bishop Brondel was bombarded with complaints about the behavior of "that black woman," and in July 1894 he ordered her to leave the mission. An indignant Mary threatened to go to Helena and confront him, but finally she bowed to the inevitable and moved into nearby Cascade. There, with Mother Amadeus's help, she opened a restaurant.

Residents soon began to glimpse a softer side of strong-willed and hot-tempered Mary. Knowing firsthand what it was like to go hungry, she served free meals to anyone unable to pay. While her benevolence won her friends, it caused her to go broke twice, and after only about ten months in the restaurant business, she was forced to quit.

Mother Amadeus then convinced officials to let Mary deliver the mail between Cascade and Saint Peter's. According to some sources, she was only the second woman postal driver in the nation. Respect for her grew as she braved blizzards, floods, and wolves to ensure that the mail got through. If the snow was too deep or the weather too cold for her horses, she shouldered the mail sacks and carried them, traveling on snowshoes. Mary, the townspeople finally acknowledged, was a "diamond in the rough."

In her seventies, Mary finally began to feel her age. She retired in 1903 from more strenuous activities and opened a laundry in Cascade—but she could still brawl with the best of them. One day, when a customer who had neglected to pay his two-dollar laundry bill passed the saloon where she was drinking, she confronted him and knocked him flat with one punch to the jaw. That account, she announced with satisfaction, was now settled in full.

Mary Fields became legendary throughout Montana. When she celebrated her birthday, the local school would close so she could treat the children to a party. She served as official mascot for the town's baseball team and was in big demand as a babysitter. When a law was passed banning women from saloons, Mayor D. W. Munroe won a friend for life when he granted Mary an exemption.

Mary died on December 5, 1914, at Columbus Hospital in Great Falls, but she lives on in memory as one of the most picturesque characters in Montana history. Cowboy artist Charles M. Russell immortalized her in his 1897 pen-and-ink sketch, "A Quiet Day in Cascade." On display at the C. M. Russell Museum in Great Falls, it shows her sitting on the ground next to an upset basket of eggs.

Perhaps the most fitting epitaph for this remarkable and unconventional woman was composed by actor and Montana native Gary Cooper in 1959. "Born a slave somewhere in Tennessee," he wrote in an article for *Ebony* magazine, "Mary lived to become one of the freest souls ever to draw a breath or a .38." ❖

MARIA DEAN

Woman of Medicine

*U*ndertakers in Helena, Montana Territory, were busier than usual in the fall of 1885. In a matter of weeks, diptheria had stormed through the capital city, snatching lives by the dozens. The rumble of horse-drawn hearses had become a familiar sound in the washboard streets, and most of them bore the undersized coffins of little children.

Dr. Maria Dean had plenty of reason to be concerned. As a physician, she mourned the loss of each and every patient. As chairwoman of the Helena Board of Health, she was responsible for controlling the epidemic. She sat at her desk and penned a polite but insistent appeal to the public. It appeared in the *Helena Daily Herald* on December 4.

> In view of the fact that diptheria exists in this city and that there are likely to be more cases developed during this month, the Board of Health ... calls the attention of the citizens to the ordinance requiring that a quarantine flag be posted up in a conspicuous place on the premises

MONTANA HISTORICAL SOCIETY, HELENA

Dr. Maria Dean

in which the case exists, and that a fine of $20 be imposed upon anyone removing it. . . . The Board would respectfully request that every attending physician do all in his power to prevent any spread of the disease, by cautioning the occupants of houses where diptheria exists to abstain from intermingling with others as far as possible, and when a case dies or recovers, to see that the bedding and premises are thoroughly disinfected and allow no bedding to be exposed to the public by being hung out on fences near the sidewalks for the purpose of airing them.

Medicine had come a long way in the twenty-seven years since Maria's birth. Only recently had doctors begun to understand about germs and contagion and the need for sanitation. And diptheria—which attacked the respiratory system causing fever, chills, sore throat, and brassy cough—was one of the most serious contagious diseases with which early day Montanans had to cope. It could damage a victim's heart or produce enough phlegm to block breathing.

As Maria Dean pleaded with the sickened city of Helena, the first effective cure for diptheria was still five years away. Still, treatment had progressed considerably from the days when snails and earthworms mashed in water was an accepted folk remedy. Or when a doctor would hold a youngster upside-down and tickle his throat with a feather soaked in goose grease to make him vomit the gunk that clogged his windpipe. Dr. Dean treated more than her share of diptheria cases that fall. She specialized in the diseases of women and children, in part because many men in those days were repulsed and embarrassed by the idea of a female doctor.

Not quite forty years had passed since the first woman in America had received a degree in medicine. A year later, in 1850, a doctor addressing the New York Medical Society voiced the sentiments of most men when he claimed that "the bare thought of married females engaging in the medical profession is palpably absurd. It carries with it a sense of shame, vulgarity, and disgust."

After all, a nineteenth-century woman was supposed to be fragile and refined. She was expected to stay home and, as one druggist put it, "look after her house and darn her husband's stockings." Doctoring was simply too nasty and intimate for the delicate sensibilities of true womanhood, most people believed, and the reputation of any woman who dared to think otherwise was likely to be tarnished.

"To be addressed in public as doctor was painful," one female physician confessed, "for all heads would turn to look at the woman thus stigmatized."

Nonetheless, a growing number of women took up stethoscopes and black bags, beginning in the 1870s. By 1880, census-takers were able to count more than two thousand registered female physicians in the United States. Nine years later, Maria became the first woman issued a license to practice medicine in the fresh new state of Montana.

Maria Morrison Dean was born in 1858 in Madison, Wisconsin, the oldest of three sisters. She graduated in 1880 from the University of Wisconsin, where her mother worked as a sorority housemother. Her uncle had been one of the founders of the university and had served for a time as its president.

No one knows what motivated Maria to choose such an unconventional career for a woman. For three years after her college graduation, she studied to be a physician at the Boston University School of Medicine. Then she sailed to Germany to continue her training. When the Berlin Opera House burned to the ground, she got a grisly, firsthand lesson on the treatment of severe burns. It wasn't long, though, before Maria returned to America and settled in Helena, probably because her younger sister, Annie, had recently moved there with her husband.

Maria began to build a large and successful practice and showed a special interest in the mentally ill, as well as in women and children. She was among the first doctors to practice at Saint Peter's Hospital after it was constructed in 1887. Maria also jumped wholeheartedly into civic and educational affairs. She served as chairwoman of the Helena Board of Education for several years and helped establish the local Young Women's Christian Association (YWCA).

Not surprisingly, Dr. Dean believed in equal rights for women and lobbied for suffrage with enthusiasm and determination. A prominent member of the Montana Equal Suffrage Association and its predecessor, the Montana Woman Suffrage Association, she played an active role in the successful 1914 campaign for the vote. Her nephew, Huntley Child, once told an interviewer that Maria was asked to run for Congress but declined. The honor went instead to fellow feminist and friend Jeannette Rankin, who became the nation's first congresswoman.

In 1918, Maria's health failed while she was visiting her sister Annie in Washington, D.C. President Woodrow Wilson, whom she had befriended during a previous visit, loaned her his private railroad car for the first leg of her final journey home. She died in Helena on May 19, 1919, and was buried beneath a tombstone inscribed "The Beloved Physician." The community, the *Helena Independent* lamented, had lost a "public-spirited" and "great-hearted" woman. ❧

ELLA KNOWLES HASKELL

Belle of the Bar

$\mathcal{E}$lla Knowles had lobbied hard for the right to practice law in Montana. But as the first female attorney in the state, she had another obstacle to overcome. She needed to drum up some business—and that wouldn't be easy given American society's strong prejudice against working women in the late 1800s.

It was common practice in Montana just before the turn of the century for young lawyers to launch their careers by collecting bad debts. So Ella hiked up and down Main Street in Helena, asking assorted businessmen if anyone owed them money, and offering to collect.

"They did not receive me well," she later recalled. "They didn't take kindly to the idea of a woman 'doing a man's work.'"

Ella began to get desperate; she had to earn a living. So one rainy day, the plucky, blue-eyed blonde hitched up her long skirts, waded through the muddy streets, and marched in the front door of one of the local shops. This time, she was determined not to take "no" for an answer. Later, she described what happened next.

Ella Knowles

I saw instantly that I was not welcome when I entered the store, but I referred to the [unpaid] bills again. Then [the merchant] showed his impatience.

"If you want to collect anything," he exclaimed, "go and collect some of my umbrellas. I own three of them; one I loaned to Mrs. So and So, and another was borrowed by Mrs. Blank weeks ago, and none of them have been returned. Here it is raining, and I cannot go to lunch because somebody has borrowed my umbrellas and did not return them."

With that he turned and walked to the rear of the store. I was vexed and chagrined. I hesitated for a moment, and then I decided to act on the suggestion he gave me, although he did not expect me to do it.

Ella confronted the two offenders on their doorsteps that very day, and though one of them "flared up" and the other gave her a withering look that haunted her in her sleep that night, they produced the umbrellas in question. She tucked them under her arm and returned to the store.

"Here are your umbrellas," she announced, "and my fee is fifty cents." She was dismayed by the merchant's reaction.

He looked shocked and dumfounded when he realized what I had done, and then became angry and started to storm even worse than the two women had. There were a number of people in the store, and I appealed to them to say if I was not entitled to my fee. When they understood the case, they all agreed with me, and then the humorous phase of the matter was recognized by my client, and he joined in the general laugh. He accepted the umbrellas, paid me my fee, consisting of two 25-cent pieces, and told me my work was satisfactory.

Later, Ella learned, the merchant "did some very earnest and sincere apologizing" to the two borrowers of his umbrellas, but their indignation didn't keep him from retaining her as his attorney from then on. She kept the two quarters for the rest of her life and sentimentally referred to them as her "mascots." It wasn't long before Montana's first woman lawyer had not only plenty of clients, but an excellent reputation as well.

Ella Knowles was born on July 31, 1860, the only child of staunch New Englanders David and Louisa Knowles. She grew up in Northwood Ridge, New Hampshire, and received her early education from her mother, who died when Ella was fourteen. At fifteen, Ella graduated from Northwood Seminary, and a year later from Plymouth State Normal School, where she trained to be a teacher. She worked for four years in neighborhood schools, then entered Bates College in Lewiston, Maine—despite the common notion that a higher education was wasted on a woman. In 1884, she became the fifth woman ever to graduate from that institution, and she did so with high honors.

After graduation, Ella moved to Manchester, New Hampshire, and began to study law at one of the local law firms. Illness forced her to quit, and in 1888 she took the advice of her doctor and moved out West, where she settled in Helena and taught school for a year. She was offered a job as a principal, but to her friends' dismay, she declined and resumed her study of law, this time in the office of Helena lawyer Joseph W. Kinsley.

The idea of female lawyers was still a novel one. The first woman attorney in the nation had been admitted to the Iowa bar in 1869, and by 1890 there were still only about fifty, many of them serving as assistants to their husbands. Society generally believed that women lacked the physical stamina and aggressive nature required by the profession. They also were considered too emotional and irrational to pursue the hard truth. Finally, people feared that the demands of the profession would interfere with a woman's "proper" role as homemaker.

"The natural and proper timidity and delicacy which belongs to the female sex unfits it for many of the occupations of civil life . . . ," wrote one U.S. Supreme Court justice. "The paramount destiny and mission of women are to fulfill the noble and benign offices of wife and mother. This is the law of the Creator."

But such sentiment wasn't enough to dissuade persistent Ella Knowles. When she learned that Montana statute prohibited women from practicing law, she began lobbying legislators to change the code. In 1889, the territorial legislature bowed to her wishes—despite some concern about inflicting "the demoralizing and degrading trials and tribulations of mankind" upon the "finer senses of the woman"—and Ella was admitted to the bar on December 26 of that year. The team of lawyers that administered the bar exam was impressed by her performance.

"Examined Miss Knowles for admission to the Bar and was surprised to find her so well read," one of them wrote in his journal. "She beat all that I have ever examined."

Ella went on to build a lucrative law practice. A majority of her clients were men. In 1907, the *Anaconda Standard* reported that "there is not a practicing attorney in the courts of Montana who is regarded with greater respect, and for whose knowledge of the law and legal ability other members of the bar have a higher regard."

Ella didn't let her professionalism interfere with her social life. She was once described as a "charming example of the eternal feminine, enjoying to the full pretty gowns, cards, and the talk and laughter of social occasions."

Ella never forgot her first court case, in which she represented a Chinese man who had been employed by a black restaurant owner. Her client had quit his job, and he claimed his boss owed him five dollars in back wages. In court, the employer produced an account book showing he had already paid his former employee. Ella was about to concede defeat when she was struck by inspiration. She examined the accounts with a magnifying glass and discovered that the crooked employer had erased and changed some of the figures. The justice of the peace ruled in favor of Ella's client.

In 1892, Ella was surprised when the grass-roots Populist Party nominated her for state attorney general. She lost by a narrow margin despite a "remarkably plucky fight," and the winning candidate, Henri J. Haskell, demonstrated his respect for her abilities by appointing her assistant attorney general in 1893. On May 23, 1895, he expressed his admiration even further by marrying her. The couple divorced a few years later.

An obvious champion of equal rights for women, Ella became president of the Montana Woman Suffrage Association in 1896. An excellent public speaker, she once explained the connection she saw between a society's treatment of women and its general well-being:

> Degrade woman, cripple her faculties, hamper her intellectual growth, and the result is a degraded, crippled, or enslaved people. . . . Elevate woman, give her full freedom to use the faculties God has given her, not as a matter of favor, but as an act of simple justice, and the result is a people strong and self-reliant, intellectual and valiant, a people of no less development than our own, able to defend the flag we love, and the advance teachers of civilized humanity.

In 1909, Ella was again plagued by poor health. With several friends, she toured the world, hoping that the rest would help her get well. The plan failed, and on January 27, 1911, she died of an infection in Butte, Montana, at the age of fifty. She left behind a large law practice and what her obituary described as a "neat fortune," as well as the esteem of attorneys and judges throughout the state and nation. ❧

Frontier Photographer

$\mathscr{E}$velyn Cameron swung out of the saddle juggling a bulky box camera, a tripod, and a stack of fragile, glass-plate negatives. She had ridden the six miles from her ranch to town at the request of one of eastern Montana's early settlers, an eccentric Irishwoman named Mrs. Collins. As Evelyn set up her camera to snap the woman's portrait, her customer announced that she could not possibly have her picture taken—not, that is, until she found her false teeth.

After a thorough search, Mrs. Collins concluded that her dog must have stolen her dentures, mistaking them, perhaps, for some exotic bone. But the fiesty pioneer was not about to give up on her photo session. Life in the hinterlands had taught her to make do.

"She wished me to go & borrow Mrs. Van Horn's [teeth], which I did," Evelyn noted in her diary on March 20, 1900. "She had to take them out & wash them first!!!"

Since her arrival in eastern Montana in 1889, Evelyn had never ceased to be impressed by the resourcefulness, pluck, and perseverance of the inhabitants of these lonely badlands. For three decades, she sought to capture this frontier spirit on film, and by the time of

Evelyn Cameron

MONTANA HISTORICAL SOCIETY, HELENA

her death in 1928, she herself had become one of its best examples—an achievement all the more remarkable given her genteel, British upbringing.

Evelyn Cameron was born Evelyn Jephson Flower on August 26, 1868, on a rambling country estate south of London. She grew up amid all the comforts of late Victorian England: servants, governesses, and nannies; high teas, cricket, and fox hunts. A half-brother, Cyril Flower, would serve in Parliament and rise into the ranks of the nobility.

Evelyn abandoned her life of luxury and decorum in 1889, when she married Ewen Cameron, a stern-looking Scot with a handle-bar mustache. Her family didn't approve of the match. Ewen was thirty-six—fifteen years older than his bride—and his health and financial prospects were shaky. Perhaps to escape her family's displeasure, the couple decided to spend their honeymoon hunting big game in the North American wilderness.

Evelyn had heard tales of the bountiful wildlife in the American West from her oldest brother, who had gone on a hunting expedition there in 1888. Eastern Montana in particular had attracted a small battalion of upper-crust Britons looking for opportunity and sport. Many of them had bought ranches and were raising horses in the Miles City area.

The Camerons arrived in Montana in the company of an English cook and a crusty guide who had once served as a scout for the ill-fated Lieutenant Colonol George Armstrong Custer. The honeymooners were favorably impressed by the rugged badlands and limitless prairie that surrounded Miles City. Although the land must have seemed empty and endless after the cozy villages and lush meadows of home, it possessed its own brand of surreal and subtle beauty. Wind and water had carved bizarre sculptures out of the local sandstone and gumbo clay, revealing muted layers of red, pink, coral, yellow, and brown. Massive cottonwoods crowded the banks of the Yellowstone River, and splashes of wildflowers created oases amid the otherwise sparse vegetation.

"Miles may be traversed with never a sign of man nor a sound more civilized than the Falcon's angry scream," Ewen wrote of the barren landscape.

Yet the Camerons liked what they saw. The air was invigorating. The open range was a vast ocean of free grass. It was an ideal place, Ewen decided, to raise polo ponies for export to Great Britain. With the financial backing of a partner, he imported a pair of Arabian stallions, expecting to make an easy fortune. Unfortunately, he proved to have a knack for making disastrous business decisions.

At first, the Camerons rented a ranch on the Powder River, east of Miles City. When the horses failed to thrive there, they moved to another ranch about six miles south of Terry, a tiny, ten-year-old community midway between Miles City and Glendive. Well-mannered Evelyn was not impressed with the rough-and-ready railroad town. In a letter to her sister-in-law, she wrote:

> Terry has been rather lively of late, cowboys shooting here, there & everywhere. One saloon is riddled with bullet holes & one cowpuncher held up the Justice of the "Piece" (this is his spelling not mine). In fact, they painted the town red & not one was arrested!

The Camerons named their new spread the Eve Ranch after the first three letters in Evelyn's name. The house, a three-room log cabin with a wooden verandah, nestled against a hillside within earshot of a gurgling creek. Although it was a far cry from the manor house in which she'd spent her childhood, Evelyn was happy there. She loved ranch life and the hard work it entailed. On September 8,

1893, she wrote in her diary, "I don't care about home [England] now, feel as tho' I would like to never hear nor go near it."

But soon it looked as though the Camerons might be forced to return to Great Britain. The polo-pony enterprise had been gobbling up their financial resources, and when their bank failed during the national recession known as the Panic of 1893, they lost what little money they had.

Evelyn refused to give up. "To return to England in financial ruin would be the ultimate indignity," she wrote. So she looked for ways to help make ends meet. She began selling vegetables from her garden to local ranchers and cowboys. She allowed her oafish brother Alec to come live with her in return for quarterly rent payments. And though it packed the tiny cabin to the bursting point, she finally took in another boarder, a well-to-do Irishman named Adams. It was he who introduced Evelyn to the art of photography and he who rode to the Terry railroad depot on August 13, 1894, to pick up the camera that Evelyn had ordered.

Evelyn had to squeeze her study of photography into days already crammed with chores. In addition to the endless churning and cooking and sewing and washing and gardening that ate up the time of most pioneer women, she also shouldered most of the tasks that were generally considered "man's work." She roped and branded cattle, dehorned calves, broke wild horses, milked cows, cleaned stables and corrals, and chopped wood. Ewen spent most of his time observing and writing about wildlife, especially birds. His sickly constitution may have kept him from doing ranch work.

Donna Lucey, Evelyn's biographer, was awed by Evelyn's prodigious labors. In her book *Photographing Montana* she wrote:

The overwhelming impression one is left with through-out Evelyn Cameron's diaries is the sheer physical and emotional strength that life in frontier Montana demanded. Work was never-ending and backbreaking and there were few distractions. Days, weeks, months might go by between town visits for Evelyn.

In her diary entry of October 7, 1899, Evelyn dispassionately described a typical day:

Arose 5:50. Jan [the dog] woke me out of a deep sleep scratching at our door to be let out. Breakfast started. Fed chicks and milked Roanie. Cut up [Roanie's] squashes and cucumbers. Breakfast at 8:40. . . . Cleaned our room. Skinned out a little horned owl for Ewen. Began to wash 12:15. Lunch 1:40. . . . Worked up sponge [yeast] into dough. . . . Made dough into loaves. Printed 5 [negative plates] and spotted plates. . . . 2 [plates] require too much doctoring [for scratches] to print from. This made me late getting washing done. 1 sheet, 7 towels, 8 dish clothes, 3 pillow cases, 2 aprons, 2 blouses, 6 flannel shirts, 2 vests, 1 pair drawers, 2 flannel combis, 4 pair socks, 1 nightgown. . . . Scrubbed floor; baked and put supper on 4:40. Fed pups. Fed chicks. Milked. . . . I churned after supper 2 lbs., 4 ounces butter. Wrote diary.

And yet Evelyn rarely complained. In fact, she relished the dangers and rigors of frontier life. "Manual labor is about all I care about," she once said in a letter to a niece, "and, after all, [that] is what will really make a strong woman."

Even Montana's severe weather couldn't defeat her. "We have the troubles of Arctic explorers out here but none of the credit," she wrote with good humor to her niece on a particularly bitter January day. On another occasion, she described a day so frigid that "anything left in the kitchen for 15 minutes will be frozen hard."

To master the rudiments of photography, Evelyn often worked until dawn developing her negatives, then moved on to her other chores at daybreak, barely stopping to rest. She focused her camera on cowboys, sheepherders, homesteaders, and wolf hunters, as well as on the spacious Montana landscape and its animal inhabitants. With no telephoto lens to rely upon, she resorted to daring and patience to take remarkable closeups of the native wildlife. Once, she climbed a steep cliff carrying her unwieldy equipment and dangled from its side so she could photograph a golden eagle's nest containing two eggs. She returned to the eyrie often after the eggs hatched to document the growth of the eaglets. According to Lucey,

> [they] became so accustomed to her calm and continuing presence that they paid little attention to her, or to Ewen, who was busily scribbling notes about their plumage and habits. . . .
>
> [H]aving won the eaglet's confidence, [she] was able to take great liberties with them, at times prodding them mercilessly until they got into the position she wanted or assumed an appropriately photogenic expression. . . . The regal birds eventually permitted her to pick them up with her bare hands and pose them. Among the images she made of them is a self-portrait with one of the birds perched on her outstretched arm.

Evelyn had a way with animals and a deep affection for them. Among the assortment of pets she kept at various times in Montana were hunting dogs, cats, lambs, antelopes, hawks, and wolf cubs. Once, after killing a mother grizzly during a hunting trip, she insisted on carrying the two orphaned cubs home with her. She kept them alive with condensed milk until she could send them via steamship to the London zoo.

On another occasion, the Camerons bought a pair of month-old wolf cubs from a professional wolf hunter. Ewen described them in a magazine article he wrote:

> They were unquestionably the most playful animals which I have ever seen, romping boisterously with each other until tired, or indulging in a grand game with any acceptable plaything such as a glove. They had soft mouths like a well trained retriever, and one of their favourite amusements was to carry about a kitten of their own age. At first my wife would rescue from their jaws the wet, slimy, mewing cat, fearing it might be hurt—more especially when both wolves had hold of it together. Such interference, however, was decidedly futile, for the kitten, as soon as it could escape, invariably returned to its waiting playfellows to be conveyed about as before.

As the wolves matured, they grew more skittish and more fierce, until Ewen finally decided they were dangerous and sent them to a zoo at Coney Island, New York.

As the Camerons' financial situation grew more and more precarious, they relied increasingly on the income from Evelyn's photography. She charged a quarter for each of her pictures or three dollars for a dozen. The money proved crucial in 1897, when the polo-pony venture finally floundered. Two years earlier, the Camerons had begun shipping their ponies abroad, but the English didn't like the wild American horses, or their unsightly brands. When six animals died as a result of their ocean voyage in 1897, the polo-pony business died with them.

In 1900, a dispirited Ewen's health began to fail. The couple decided to return to Britain for two years so that he could get better medical care. But Evelyn couldn't stand the slow pace of life in the English countryside.

"She went nearly mad with the forced inactivity," Lucey wrote. "Teatime did not compare to ranching in her estimation, and the gentle meadows of England offered none of the adventure she found in Montana."

So, one year later, the Camerons returned and built a new Eve Ranch on fourteen hundred acres fourteen miles from Terry. In 1907, they would move to a fourth ranch within sight of the Yellowstone River. Evelyn would spend the rest of her life there.

Ewen's health careened downhill. By 1915, he was unable to leave his bed and lapsed into endless renditions of the song "It's a Long Way to Tipperary." Evelyn nursed him until he died on May 25, 1915. An autopsy revealed he had cancer of the liver and brain.

From then on, Evelyn ran the ranch alone, "as busy as a one-armed man with hives," as she put it. But she was content with her life; and her generosity, compassion, resourcefulness, independence, and hard work earned her the admiration of her neighbors. A traveling Englishwoman once called her "the most respected, most talked of woman in the whole of the state.

"Never was [Evelyn] described as English or American by her admirers," the woman wrote in 1919. "They just called her a Montanan, and no better description could be found for her, for she is the very embodiment of the spirit of that great state."

In 1918, Evelyn cemented her bond to Montana by becoming a U.S. citizen. Ten years later, on the day after Christmas, she died of heart failure after a routine appendectomy. Even death she saw as an adventure. She once wrote, "I think of death as a delightful journey that I shall take when all my tasks are done."

Fortunately for the generations that would follow her, Evelyn Cameron left behind a remarkable legacy: thirty-five leather-bound diaries and thousands of photographs—in Lucey's words, "a virtual home movie of life on the frontier."

Yet Evelyn might well have been forgotten if not for Lucey. In 1978, the New York editor was hunting for photographs to illustrate a book on pioneer women when she came across a few of Cameron's striking images at the Montana Historical Society. A staff member told her that an elderly woman in eastern Montana—a longtime friend of Evelyn—was rumored to have a large collection of negatives stored in her basement. With great patience, Lucey convinced the woman to share the treasure, an experience she said was "like opening King Tut's tomb."

Since then, many of Evelyn's photos—as well as other mementoes of her life—have been exhibited throughout Montana. They reveal an exceptional woman whose spirit, Lucey notes, "could not be contained even by the Big Sky country she settled." ❧

Fra Dana

Star-Crossed Impressionist

*W*hen Fra Dana moved to Wyoming with her mother and half-sister in 1893, she was already a promising young artist who dared to dream of fame. But in Wyoming she would discover a second passion—one that would wrench her away from her paints and brushes. Torn between the two, she would spend the rest of her life watching her artistic ambitions wither.

Born on November 26, 1874, in Terre Haute, Indiana, Fra (pronounced Fray) had a somewhat unsettled though affluent childhood. Her parents, John and Julia Broadwell, divorced—a difficult and shocking event in those days of Victorian values. Her mother's second husband, James Dinwiddie, died when Fra was fifteen.

That same year, Fra enrolled at the Cincinnati Art Academy and began studying painting under the well-known artist J. H. Sharp, best known for his portraits of famous Native Americans. Her work impressed him so much that he once pronounced her one of the finest artists he knew. "She paints like a man!" he gushed in what was meant to be the ultimate compliment.

But that Fra was not a man was the crux of her dilemma. Women

COURTESY OF HARRIET KERNS

Fra Dana

of the early twentieth century were expected to settle comfortably into the roles of wife and mother. They were not encouraged to pursue their own careers. It was difficult—sometimes even impossible—for a woman to juggle the responsibilities of work and home, as Fra was about to find out for herself.

When Fra's stepfather died, she moved with her mother and half-sister to some land the Dinwiddies owned near Parkman, Wyoming, a few miles south of the Montana border. There, she met Edwin L. Dana, a successful and charismatic cattle rancher ten years her senior. They married on July 1, 1896, but only after Edwin promised that Fra could continue to study art.

A year after the wedding, Fra held him to his prenuptial agreement. She enrolled at the Art Institute in Chicago and, later, at the Art Students League in New York, where she worked under the tutelage of the noted painter William Merritt Chase. She went on to Paris to study with avant-garde artists Mary Cassatt and Alfred Maurer. Edwin stayed behind to run their flourishing ranch, which lay at the foot of the Bighorn Mountains, straddling the Montana-Wyoming border.

Fra painted vigorously until 1912, when increasing resistance from her husband prompted her to set aside her brushes and take a more active part in the management of the ranch. She served as Edwin's secretary and bookkeeper and even rode the range and helped with the branding on occasion. According to Dennis Kern, curator of the University of Montana Museum of Fine Arts,

> she was as involved in the ranch as he was. While a part of her was very genteel and cultured, there were times when she had to put on waders and wade through the manure in the barnyard. It was a business partnership. . . . That was a tough occupation and may have pre-empted her from becoming an artist.

FRA DANA

Fra had ambivalent feelings about her life in the West. On the one hand, the ranch's prosperity enabled her to travel to Mexico, Egypt, and Europe and to assemble a fine collection of jewelry, furniture, and china. On the other hand, her husband's objections squelched her dream of becoming a successful artist. During one of Fra's visits to Paris, Mary Cassatt advised her to be "ruthless" and leave her husband. But Fra resigned herself to life with Edwin, though not without regrets. In September 1911, she made this bitter entry in her journal:

> If my life is to be bounded by Pass Creek, how can I stand it? I am full enough of life to want friends, music, painting, the theater; all the stimulus of modern movements. . . .
>
> I could fight the world and conquer, but I cannot fight the world and Edwin, too. He will always pull against me in the life that I desire. So I shall give up. He has won. I will never bother him anymore with my desires or ambitions. Why struggle? I will . . . try to content myself with the flowers and the books.

With Fra's help, the Dana Ranch grew until, in 1918, it was reputed to be the largest purebred Hereford operation in the nation. About six thousand cattle grazed the Dana's 400,000-acre range, which spilled onto the Crow Indian reservation. That same year, the couple expanded their operation with the lease and purchase of about 64,000 acres in central Montana, just south of Great Falls. Edwin retired to the Montana ranch in 1937, but Fra, whose health was failing, chose to live in an apartment in the nearby city. There, she resumed her painting at last, and it was during this final stage of her life that she produced her best work.

UNIVERSITY OF MONTANA, MUSEUM OF FINE ARTS COLLECTION

Dana's self portrait entitled On the Window Seat

Fra's paintings—primarily still lifes and portraits rendered in oils—reflect the influence of her early teachers, some of whom were among America's best impressionists. One of her works, a self-portrait entitled *On the Window Seat*, contains "more than a whisper of impressionist techniques," according to Kern. In it, Fra has portrayed herself reading the newspaper beside a window framed with masses of spring-green foliage. Kern describes the piece as a "metaphor for her loneliness and for hope. In the painting, she leans out of the gray shadows toward the warmth and light outside."

In 1947, Fra donated her art collection—about forty-five paintings of her own, as well as several by Sharp, Chase, and Maurer—to the University of Montana Museum of Fine Arts in Missoula. Thirty-five years later, Kern discovered the collection hidden away in storage and recognized it for the "real treasure" it is. Since then, he has prepared a touring exhibit that has hung in galleries throughout Montana.

Kern sees in Fra's work a distinctive talent superior even to that of the famous Montana artist Charles M. Russell. But he also sees Fra's limitations.

"All of the people she knew kind of regarded her as a hobby painter, and I know that was very frustrating for her," he said. "She was actually a very good artist. The only reservation I have is that she didn't paint more. If she had painted more, I think she could have been a major figure in American art. Certainly the ability was there, and the vision."

Fra didn't live to see her work get the recognition it deserved. She died of cancer in Great Falls in 1948. When the university asked her for biographical information to accompany her art collection, her reply was brief, humble, and tinged with remorse. "I do not know that there is anything to tell you about my life. My annals are short and simple. I was born, I married, I painted a little, I am ready to die." ⚜

FANNY CORY COONEY

Mother First, Artist Second

*L*ike many a would-be artist, Fanny Cory trudged the streets of New York City with her portfolio tucked under her arm. She was making the rounds of the big-league publishers, hoping to land her first job as a professional illustrator. At the door of an old brick building in the Bowery, she paused to marshal her courage. Then, heart pounding, she climbed the stairs to the third floor, where the prestigious Harper Publishing Company had its offices in the late 1890s.

After wandering a few dim corridors, Fanny finally found the office she was seeking. She opened the door marked "Art Department" and peeped inside. The occupant of the room, a man in a blush-colored shirt, was slouched behind a massive desk, busily filing his fingernails. In a small voice, Fanny introduced herself and laid her drawings before him.

The man riffled through the pile, barely glancing at the sketches. "You are a student?" he asked.

"Yes," she timidly replied.

With a sneer, he tossed her drawings back at her. "You must

PHOTOGRAPHED BY AND COURTESY OF BOB COONEY

Fanny Cory Cooney

get yourself a reputation," he said, "before you come here."

Later, Fanny recalled that she stalked out "boiling mad." But she eventually got the last laugh, for she would go on to become one of the finest illustrators of children's books and magazines in the first half of the twentieth century. Soon, the Harper company would gladly buy several of her drawings for its popular periodical *Harper's Bazaar*.

Fortunately, Fanny didn't let her first rejection ruin her resolve. She moved on to the next publisher, and the next, until finally she hit paydirt at the office of *Century Magazine*. Years later, her children remembered the story she would tell about her first sale.

"I was rather nervously showing some little pen and ink drawings to Mr. Drake, the editor of the *Century Magazine*," she would say. "He seemed to like one and marked $25.00 on the margin. As I remember I gasped and said, 'Oh, that's too much.' He obligingly erased the figure and put down $20.00. Anyway, that was the beginning of a very pleasant relationship with that magazine and many others."

Fanny Young Cory was born in Waukegan, Illinois, in 1877, but she would spend most of her adult life on a ranch thirty miles east of Helena, Montana, near a place called Canyon Ferry. Her mother, Jessie McDougall Cory, died of tuberculosis when Fanny was ten. Her father, Benjamin Sayre Cory, was a traveling salesman who seldom stayed at home. His grandson once described him as "a cantankerous little man" who "apparently provided rather poorly for his family." Fanny was the youngest of four Cory children who survived to adulthood. Two brothers died when they were young.

A year before their mother's death, Fanny's older brother Bob succumbed to gold fever and headed to Montana in search of a cure. In 1889, he invited his father and sisters to join him in Helena. Fanny's older sister, Agnes, traveled to Montana Territory with their father, but for some forgotten reason Fanny went alone by train. The petite twelve-year-old cradled a doll in her lap, hoping the other passengers would think she was a grown woman with a baby.

In Helena, Fanny discovered that she didn't care much for school—except, that is, for an art class taught by Mary Wheeler, a painter trained in Boston and Paris. Fanny had begun doodling even as a preschooler, often lying on the floor of the kitchen so absorbed in her work that her family had to step over her. Miss Wheeler believed Fanny had talent and urged her to get formal artistic training.

Fanny got the chance to do just that in 1894, when her brother Jack and his wife invited her and Agnes to stay with them in New York City, where Jack had established himself as a political cartoonist. Two years later, Fanny enrolled in the Metropolitan School of Art and the following year in the prestigious Art Students League.

Fanny worried that she was a burden to her brother, so when she was twenty she quit art school and set out to make her living in the big city. She intended to care for her beloved sister Agnes, an invalid who had contracted tuberculosis while caring for their mother. But Agnes died in her sister's arms that year, hurtling Fanny into a dangerous depression. Her brothers took her camping in Montana for the summer to try to cheer her up.

Fanny didn't have to tramp the streets of New York long before joining the ranks of professional artists. By the turn of the century, her whimsical drawings of children were romping across the covers and through the pages of some of the most popular magazines of the time, including *Scribner's, Century, Harper's Bazaar, Liberty,* and the *Saturday Evening Post.* Her work also began to brighten books. From 1899 through 1902, she illustrated ten novels, including her own version of *Alice's Adventures in Wonderland* and several books by L. Frank Baum, creator of the Land of Oz.

By 1902, Fanny had tired of New York and decided to return to Montana. She and her brothers each built a little cabin on Beaver Creek northeast of Helena, where Fanny continued to work as a prominent illustrator. When she wasn't drawing or painting, she was fishing, hunting, riding, golfing, bicycling, and skating. It was during picnics on Beaver Creek and skating parties at Canyon Ferry Lake (known then as Sewell Lake) that she got to know Fred Cooney, son of one of the local pioneers. They married in the spring of 1904 and lived for almost fifty years at the Cooney ranch on the lake's east shore.

For a few years after her wedding, Fanny continued to work under her maiden name, but soon her artistic career skidded almost to a halt so that she could devote herself to an entirely different creative endeavor. After years of bringing children to life on paper, Fanny wanted some flesh-and-blood children of her own. Thirteen would be nice, she once told an interviewer.

In 1905, Fanny went into labor with her first baby, but the delivery went tragically awry. The infant son died at birth, and Fanny barely survived. Her doctor warned her that future pregnancies could kill her.

But Fanny was persistent—as her early rounds in New York suggested. She ignored the doctor's grave advice and gave birth to a healthy daughter, Sayre, in 1907. Sons Bob and Ted soon joined the household, in 1909 and 1910.

For the next two decades, Fanny devoted herself to her children with the same passion, drive, and confidence that had brought her success as an artist. As son Bob later explained, "Mother practically abandoned the place she had earned in the art world to become a full-time mother and ranch wife." This was no easy task in a home with no plumbing, no electricity, and no automatic washer to handle the towers of dirty diapers. If Fanny resented giving up her career to read Tarzan stories by the light of a kerosene lamp, her children never knew it. In 1951, she would be named Montana Mother of the Year, an honor she would always treasure.

In the 1920s and 1930s, hard times hit the Cooney ranch, and there was no money to pay for college educations. Fanny wanted the best for her children, so she decided to dig out her pens and paintbrushes to help feed the family coffers.

"I soon found that my pet field of illustrating had been overrun with women far cleverer than myself," she later told a reporter. "Being so far from the publishers was another handicap. . . . I tried hard to think up something new."

"Say, Muvver, can't Baby stop playin' her's a geyser while her is eatin' her bread an' milk?"

"Nobody seems to be waitin on me berry much in iss store."

"Whoo-hoo! Muvver, here's a feavver in Baby's hair! What you fink? Chicken-pox?"

Samples of F.Y. Cory's Sonnysayings *newspaper cartoons*

Brother Jack, the cartoonist, suggested that Fanny try her hand at newspaper comics. So she sat down at her drawing board and created Sonny, a precocious pee-wee philosopher with curly locks and a zestful approach to life that was guaranteed to draw a smile. In 1926, the *Philadelphia Ledger Syndicate* began distributing the daily cartoon, which Fanny dubbed "Sonnysayings." Once described as an early day "Family Circus," it delighted readers for thirty years. "Home work comes in kind'a handy," read the caption of the January 19, 1932, panel. "I alers does mine right after supper so Baby has t' wipe the dishis 'stead oh me!"

Many of five-year-old Sonny's cutesy quips and antics sprang from Fanny's memories of her children's early years. But as the comic strip spread to papers across the nation and abroad—including

Norway, Australia, Canada, and Mexico—friends, neighbors, and readers began to contribute words of wisdom from the mouths of their own babes.

"One lady assured me that she had been almost standing over her two little girls with pencil and notebook in hand, waiting for bright or precocious remarks," Fanny once said, "but that 'The dumb little things never said a word worth writing down.'"

By 1929, Sonny was so popular that E. P. Dutton published a collection of the cartoons in book form. Six years later, Fanny began a new strip, *Little Miss Muffet*, designed to compete with the popular *Little Orphan Annie*. Sometimes, when the weather was bad, her husband Fred had to ride horseback to the post office at Canyon Ferry so that Sonny and Muffet wouldn't miss their deadlines.

When she wasn't engrossed in her comics, Fanny began a series of watercolors she called "The Fairy Alphabet." Each of the twenty-six paintings, which depicted fanciful fairies and other mythical folk, was accompanied by a bit of rhyme. Although the work languished in a bureau drawer during Fanny's lifetime, it was published in 1991 under the title *The Fairy Alphabet of F. Y. Cory*. Fanny considered it her best work.

After her husband's death in 1946, Fanny lived alone for ten years at the Cooney ranch on Canyon Ferry Lake. Then, her eyesight failing, she retired from her second art career and moved to Camano Island in Washington State to live in a beachfront cottage across the road from her daughter. Despite her vision problems, she began to dabble in oils, inspired by the majestic Olympic Mountains she could see from her window.

Fanny died in 1972 at the age of ninety-four. In a tribute to his mother, Bob Cooney wrote:

> There was no overwhelming feeling of grief that bright summer morning at her burial service in the Helena Valley.

FANNY CORY COONEY

We were there to honor a caring little person who never used her talents to gain acclaim for herself, but always for the benefit of those dear to her. . . .

I am sure we were all thinking of little children tripping so joyously from her busy pen, through all those years. ❧

MONTANA HISTORICAL SOCIETY, HELENA

Nancy Cooper Russell

NANCY COOPER RUSSELL

Woman Behind the Man

*N*ancy Cooper hustled around the steamy kitchen, help-ing "Ma" Roberts set the table and put the final touches on a special meal. Mr. Roberts was due home any minute, and he had sent word that he was bringing a dinner guest.

A jangle of spur rowels on the back porch signaled the arrival of the hungry pair. Ben Roberts breezed into the kitchen, followed by a sturdy cowboy who stopped short when he saw the pretty seventeen-year-old girl who had joined the Roberts household since his last visit. Mrs. Roberts introduced Nancy to their guest: Charlie Russell, former cowpuncher, fledgling artist, and close friend of the family. Nancy, she explained, had come to live with the Robertses in Cascade, Montana, to help care for their three children and do some of the housework.

Some say it was love at first sight. For the rest of the evening, Charlie was unusually gregarious, regaling his hosts with story after story of life in the good old days, when the West was still wild. Nancy was obviously enchanted. Thirty-four years after their introduction in October 1895, she described her first impression of this dashing maverick who would change her life:

> The picture that is engraved on my memory of him is of a man a little above average height and weight, wearing a soft shirt, a Stetson hat on the back of his blonde head, tight trousers, held up by a "half-breed sash" that clung just above the hip bones, high-heeled riding boots on very small, arched feet. His face was Indian-like, square jaw and chin, large mouth, tightly closed firm lips, the under protruding slightly beyond the short upper, straight nose, high cheek bones, gray-blue deep-set eyes that seemed to see everything, but with an expression of honesty and understanding. . . . His hands were good-sized, perfectly shaped, with long, slender fingers. He loved jewelry and always wore three or four rings. . . . Everyone noticed his hands, but it was not the rings that attracted, but the artistic, sensitive hands that had great strength and charm. When he talked, he used them a lot to emphasize what he was saying, much as an Indian would do.

Charlie began spending a lot of time at the Roberts home, courting the sweet-faced, buxom lass whom everyone called Mamie. In the evenings, the pair would stroll along the bank of the Missouri River and out onto the wooden bridge that spanned it, talking and gazing at the fiery colors of the sunset reflected in the muddy current. Charlie proved just how captivated he was when he gave Nancy his beloved pinto, Monte.

Everyone warned the pair not to marry. The local doctor told Charlie that Nancy had frequent fainting spells—the sign, he said, of a bad heart. He predicted she'd be dead within three years. Folks reminded Nancy that Charlie had a drinking problem. On top of that, he was fourteen years older than she and a footloose bachelor who might well be set in his ways. And he'd never managed to make a decent living for himself. How could he ever be expected to provide for a family?

But, as Charlie might have said, love is as blind as a bear in a blizzard. He proposed to Nancy, an event later recounted by his nephew Austin Russell.

It took Charlie months to make up his mind, and when he finally asked Nancy she refused. He took her for a walk at sunset, they went down by the river and crossed the echoing, wooden bridge, and on the bridge he proposed, and she said No.

Years afterward, he made a little watercolor of it—an autumn evening, the sky darkening to night, a cold wind blowing and they have just left the bridge. Nancy, downcast, is walking in front with her hands in a muff, her coat buttoned up tight and a little black hat on her head. Charlie following close behind with his coat blown open and sash and white shirt showing . . . his arms extended in a pleading, persuading, arguing gesture, his hat on the back of his head. That's all there is to it; not much of a picture, but it tells the story.

In the end, of course, she said Yes.

Charlie and Nancy were married at twilight on September 9, 1896, in the parlor of the Roberts home. Charlie had slicked himself up for the occasion, and Nancy wore a blue wedding gown that Mrs. Roberts had helped her make, along with a matching string of blue beads—her wedding gift from Charlie.

After the ceremony, the handful of guests celebrated with cake and ice cream while the newlyweds went on their "honeymoon." It was a short trip. The couple walked hand in hand about three hundred feet to the one-room shack that the Roberts had loaned Charlie for a studio. Charlie had spent almost all the money he had fixing it up to be their first home. In fact, according to Austin Russell, the pair started their life together with only about seventy-five dollars between them.

Despite everyone's reservations, Mr. and Mrs. Charles M. Russell would stay devoted to each other for the next thirty years. And Nancy would have a profound impact on the course of Charlie's artistic career. Charlie himself later acknowledged in his own quaint fashion, "The lady I trotted in double harness with was the best booster an' pardner a man ever had. . . . If it hadn't been for Mamie I wouldn't have a roof over my head."

Today, some historians go even further. If the pair hadn't married, one of them contends, "it is doubtful that Russell would have created the prodigious body of artwork he did, a life's work that is truly one of our most cherished national treasures."

Nancy Cooper was born on May 4, 1878, in Mannsville, Kentucky, a town named for her great-great-grandfather. Her mother, Texas Annie Mann, had married young, which proved to be a disastrous mistake. Nancy's father, James Al Cooper, abandoned his pregnant wife within months of the wedding, so the mother-to-be moved back to her parents' home and resumed her maiden name.

As soon as Nancy could walk, she joined her mother and grandparents working in the family tobacco fields, plucking worms off the leafy plants. When she was five, she contracted diptheria, from which she barely recovered. For the rest of her life, her health would be fragile.

In 1884, Nancy's mother was married again, this time to her

cousin James Thomas Allen, who had just come back to Kentucky after trying his hand at prospecting in Montana. Allen wanted no part of another man's child, so Nancy continued to live with her grandparents until her grandfather died and her step-grandmother went home to her family.

Nancy rejoined her mother in 1888, the same year her half-sister, Ella, was born. Two years later, Allen bundled his family onto a train and headed west to Helena, Montana, in search of a fortune in gold. When he had no luck finding a mining claim, he left his family behind and moved on to Idaho, dreaming of silver. He would send for them, he said, when he got established.

Life was hard for Texas Annie and her daughters with no one to provide for them. Mrs. Allen tried to earn a living with her sewing, while Nancy got a job doing domestic chores for fifty cents a day. One winter evening, she came home from work to find her mother in bed, burning with fever and coughing in fits. For the next nine months, she watched Texas Annie waste away until finally, when Nancy was sixteen, her once-lovely mother died of tuberculosis. Friends sent word to Allen, who returned to Helena just long enough to fetch Ella and take her back to Idaho. Nancy was left to fend for herself.

With the help of sympathetic friends, Nancy got a job with the Roberts family in Cascade, twenty-five miles southwest of Great Falls. They treated her so much like family that she called them Ma and Pa Roberts. Through them she met the most important man in her life.

About a year after their wedding, Nancy convinced Charlie to move to Great Falls, where there would be a bigger market for his paintings and sculptures. Charlie had quit the cowboy life and started trying to make a living as an artist only about three years earlier, and so far business was not exactly booming. A big part of the problem was Charlie's sociable nature. His buddies were always dropping in for a chat, or he was wandering over to the Mint or Silver Dollar Saloon for a friendly drink with the boys. He was too modest to ask people to buy his work—anyone who did was a "sucker." Instead, he gave many of his paintings away as gifts or used them as currency to pay his bills at the bars and grocery stores. Money was scarce, but Charlie was used to living on slim rations.

Nancy was more ambitious. She believed in her husband's talent and saw in it a ticket to prosperity. According to Russell biographer Harold McCracken,

> from the beginning she rode herd on him in an effort to keep him from spending too much time in the local saloon. . . . The bitter memories of her own parents' wrecked marriage had unquestionably left their mark—and a deep desire to find happiness and security for herself. . . .
>
> When [Charlie] was working on a picture and some of his former cronies dropped in for a visit or to invite him downtown for one-or-two [drinks], she refused to let them into the house or Charlie out. For this determined behavior, Nancy Russell was soon heartily disliked among some of the characters around Great Falls.

Though Charlie no doubt missed these gabfests with his friends, he conceded that Nancy had his best interests at heart. "If she hadn't prodded me," he said, "I wouldn't have done the work I did."

One day, Charles Schatzlein, a Butte storekeeper who had sold some of Charlie's pictures, stopped by the modest Russell home with a notion that would prove profitable for both Montana and American art. In *Good Medicine*, a collection of Charlie's letters that she edited after his death, Nancy recalled the man's advice:

"Do you know, Russell," he said, "you don't ask enough for your pictures. That last bunch you sent me, I sold one for enough to pay for six. I am paying you your price, but it's not enough. I think your wife should take hold of that end of the game and help you out."

From that time, the prices of Charlie's work began to advance until it was possible to live a little more comfortably.

Oddly enough, Nancy found that the higher she priced Charlie's paintings, the more people seemed to want them. Instead of the twenty-five dollars or so that Charlie had gotten for his oils, Nancy began asking—and getting—hundreds of dollars. Charlie admitted to his friends that he was embarrassed by Nancy's boldness and shocked when people paid the prices she asked. But he also had to admit that his reputation was growing. Schatzlein had judged correctly. Charlie had the soft heart, but Nancy had the head for business.

Eventually, Nancy realized that Montana was no place to make one's name and fortune as an artist. There simply weren't enough people there who could afford to invest in art. So she began to wrangle exhibitions in some of the nation's major cities: first in Saint Louis, Charlie's hometown, then in Chicago and Denver, and finally in New York.

Though Charlie hated this place he called "the big camp" with "too many tepees," New Yorkers loved his realistic renderings of life among the cowboys and Indians of what was fast becoming the Old West. In 1911, Charlie exhibited at the prestigious Folsom Galleries in New York and in 1914 at the Dore Gallery in London. To Nancy's awe and delight, the Russells were soon dining with European nobility. They would never have to worry about money again.

By now the Russells had moved into a spacious two-story home in one of Great Falls' most respectable neighborhoods. Today, the white clapboard house on Fourth Avenue North is the nucleus of the C. M. Russell Museum complex. The Russells also built a lodge on spectacular Lake McDonald in Glacier National Park. They would spend almost every summer at this place, which they called Bull's Head Lodge for the symbol with which Charlie signed his art.

There was still one thing missing from the Russells' life, and Charlie especially felt the void. In 1916, when he was fifty-two and Nancy thirty-eight, they adopted an infant they named Jack. Nancy was not an attentive mother. She often was out of town on business, and when she was home she seemed to have little patience with childish wants and needs. Much of the time, she left Jack in the care of friend and neighbor Josephine Trigg, though she tried to compensate by giving him all the material things she thought a boy could want. Charlie, on the other hand, doted on his son and, in Nancy's opinion, hopelessly spoiled him.

The Russells were now more prosperous than even Nancy had ever dreamed. But, according to author McCracken,

> success carried Charlie and his wife further and further apart in their respective conceptions of what were the most important things in life. . . . [T]he fruits of good fortune were much more appetizing to her than to him. Although Charlie's paintings were bringing prices running into five figures, she still rode herd on him with as unrelenting persistence as she had in the hungry days when they had first come to Great Falls.

By now, Charlie had spent close to sixty years in the saddle, and he was nearing the end of the trail. Yet, even when he began to complain of feeling poorly, Nancy kept him at his easel. Soon Charlie was diagnosed with goiter, an enlargement of the thyroid gland, but he refused to undergo surgery. He wasn't about to let anyone "slit his throat," as he put it. When he finally consented to an operation at the Mayo Clinic in Rochester, Minnesota, it was too late. The goiter had already damaged his heart, and his doctor predicted he had three months to live. Charlie made the man promise not to tell Nancy, but she already knew—she had instructed the doctor to keep the bad news from Charlie. They went home pretending for each other's sake that all would be well.

On October 24, 1926, Charlie Russell died of a heart attack while checking on his sleeping ten-year-old son. Nancy devoted the rest of her life to promoting his work, even refusing two marriage proposals so that she could remain Mrs. Charles M. Russell. She moved to Pasadena, California, where she died on May 23, 1940, after suffering a stroke and developing bronchial pneumonia. She was buried by Charlie's side in Great Falls.

Cowboy actor William S. Hart, a longtime friend of the Russells, once offered a touching tribute to the couple's devotion: "One could never say Charlie without saying Nancy, too, for they were always together—a real man and a real woman." ❧

FANNIE SPERRY STEELE

Champion Bronc Rider

On September 1, 1912, the most ambitious rodeo of its time got off to a sour start. A steady drizzle soaked the corrals and exhibition grounds at Victoria Park in Calgary, Alberta, where the first Calgary Stampede was about to get underway. Cowboys in rain slickers hustled to and fro on the backs of dripping mounts. Supply wagons and milling livestock churned through the mud.

As twenty-five-year-old Fannie Sperry and her mother Rachel gamely inspected the displays—including exact replicas of Old Fort Whoop-Up and the original Hudson's Bay Company trading post— a man burst out of one of the horse barns, shouting for a doctor. But it was too late. Cowboy Joe Lamar had just been thrown and trampled to death by a bronc with the deceptively innocuous name of Red Wing. Though she didn't know it, Fannie would soon have her own confrontation with the murderous beast.

Fannie Sperry had not come to Calgary to sit demurely on the sidelines and applaud the action. She had been invited to compete for the title of "Lady Bucking Horse Champion of the World." And she had every intention of winning.

THE LITTLE RED SCHOOLHOUSE, HELENA

Fannie Sperry Steele

The final day of the Stampede dawned clear and sunny. More than sixty thousand people crowded into the stands and watched as the Duke of Connaught—Governal General of Canada and uncle of the King of England—rode into the arena in an open coach pulled by two white horses. Wearing a uniform smothered in medals and a naval officer's hat crowned with a plume, he climbed into the royal box with his wife and daughter and settled down to watch the performance.

The male bronc riders went first, followed by exhibitions of stagecoach driving and rope tricks. Then came the finals of the women's bronc-riding competition. Each participant drew a slip of paper from a hat to determine which animal she would ride. Fannie drew the killer horse, Red Wing.

A more timid soul would have cringed at the prospect of climbing onto the back of one of the most dangerous horses in the bucking string, but Fannie was delighted. If she could stick to Red Wing, surely she would deserve the championship!

Fannie waited nervously as her competitors burst from the chutes atop a series of seething mounts. Finally it was her turn. The best, one of the judges announced, had been saved for last. Fannie Sperry of Mitchell, Montana, would attempt to ride the deadly bronc. Writer Dee Marvine described what happened next:

> The glistening sorrel stood taut, and a shudder rippled across his flanks as Fannie eased into the saddle. Positioning the toes of her boots in the stirrups, she adjusted her grip on the buck rein. The familiar feel of her own saddle provided small comfort, as she poised her body against the cantle, her legs gripping the horse's girth. She signaled, and the gate opened.
>
> The ride that followed is recorded in rodeo annals as

one of the best ever made by a woman—or a man. Fannie rode the murderous horse, never losing control, never sacrificing balance and style. When the hazer pulled her free in front of the royal box, a thundering ovation measured her triumph. She saluted the audience with a bow and a wide sweep of her hat.

The judges' decision was quick in coming. The first Lady Bucking Horse Champion of the World was none other than Fannie Sperry! Along with the title went a check for one thousand dollars, a gold buckle, a saddle hand-tooled with roses—and a reputation that would change her life.

Fannie Sperry was born March 27, 1887, in the shadow of the Bear Tooth, a mountain north of Helena, Montana Territory, that has since become known as the Sleeping Giant. Along with two brothers and two sisters, she grew up on the family ranch and was infected early on by her mother's love of horses. Even as a toddler, she later said, it was obvious which way her "twig was bent." Her mother often liked to tell the story of the day little Fannie waited by a spring, hoping one of the wild horses that roamed the hills behind the homestead would come to drink. When a maverick pinto approached, the toddler wielded a long scarf for a lasso and vowed to "tetch me a white-face horthie!" By the age of six, Fannie had a pony of her own.

Rachel Sperry had a no-nonsense way of teaching her children to ride. She simply plopped them onto the back of a gentle horse and told them not to fall off. If they disregarded the command, she gave them a smart smack on the behind and lifted them back into the saddle. By the time the Sperry children were teenagers, they were all expert riders capable of breaking and shoeing their own horses.

Fannie first rode for a paying audience in the summer of 1903,

THE LITTLE RED SCHOOLHOUSE, HELENA

The Montana Girls in 1907, (left to right) Anna Pauls, Christine Synness, Violet Keagle, and Fannie Sperry.

when she was only sixteen. She thrilled residents of Mitchell, a tiny settlement not far from the Sperry ranch, by sticking like a cockle-bur to the back of a writhing, white stallion. Her black braids and free right hand swung like horsewhips as the animal tried to buck her off. Onlookers were so impressed that they passed a hat and gave her all the money that was collected.

A year later, Fannie began her professional riding career—not as a bronc rider, but as a relay racer. Patterned after the Pony Express race that Buffalo Bill Cody incorporated into his Wild West show, the relays thrilled audiences in Helena, Butte, Anaconda, and Missoula. The racers changed horses several times, riding each animal an equal distance. Sometimes they had to change their own saddles. Because the riders mounted and dismounted at high speed, the threat of spills and accidents kept tension—and interest—high.

In the summer of 1905, a Butte, Montana, show promoter contracted with Fannie and three other girls to ride relay races throughout the Midwest. Billed as the "Montana Girls," they were scheduled to perform in Butte before heading east. The day before the relay races, the manager of the Butte show talked Fannie into riding an "outlaw" bronc known as Tracy. Unfortunately, the local newspaper later reported, "she had about as much chance to ride Tracy as [boxer] Jim Jeffries would have of earning a decision in a bout with a circular saw." The horse bolted out of the chute, ran about 150 yards, and stopped dead, catapulting Fannie over his head. According to the *Butte Miner*,

> she made several revolutions in the air, and then struck the ground with a dull thud. Women screamed, for it seemed that the frail equestrienne had been dashed to death. But Miss Sperry arose gamely, and approached the black demon, who had become entangled with the bridle reins, and was savagely pawing up the dirt in an effort to extricate himself. It was a rare exhibition of grit, and two thousand voices howled their approval.

Fannie had every intention of remounting the wild-eyed bronc, but men in the arena wouldn't allow it. Instead, they put a cowboy on the horse, and the show continued.

Fannie was one of only about a dozen women daring enough to ride bucking horses professionally just after the turn of the century. And she was one of only a tiny handful who rode "slick and clean," without hobbling the stirrups. Women bronc riders often tied their stirrups together with a cinch strap under the horse's belly, making it far more difficult to be thrown out of the saddle. Some considered it a less competitive way to ride. As Fannie put it, "it isn't giving the horse a fifty-fifty chance—fifty per cent in favor of him that he'll buck you off, fifty per cent in favor of you that you'll ride him." She also considered it too dangerous. With the stirrups hobbled, a rider couldn't kick free in time if a horse began to rear over backward, increasing the chances that she would be crushed beneath it.

Fannie went on to win many accolades in her riding career. In 1912, the same year as her triumph at the Calgary Stampede, she teamed up with a partner—a thirty-four-year-old cowpuncher and part-time rodeo clown named Bill Steele. She met Bill while performing at a county fair in Deer Lodge, Montana, and she married him only a few months later, on April 30, 1912. They spent their honeymoon on the rodeo circuit.

It was in Sioux City, Iowa, during the second rodeo that the Steeles entered together, that Fannie received the most serious injuries of her career. Her steed stumbled, pinning her beneath it. "She arose from the ground immediately and stood uncertainly on her feet for a moment," the *Sioux City Journal* reported, "then fainted in the arms of her husband." A badly sprained back and hip kept her out of competition for several weeks. Yet, at her first show after her convalescence—a Frontier Days celebration in Winnipeg, Manitoba—she won her second women's world bucking horse championship.

What motivated Fannie to devote herself to so dangerous a sport? After all, she stood only five feet, seven inches tall, weighed about 120 pounds, and was described as "lithe, supple, and graceful." She once justified her obsession this way:

> How can I explain to dainty, delicate women what it is like to climb down into a rodeo chute onto the back of a wild horse? How can I tell them it is a challenge that lies deep in the bones—a challenge that may go back to

prehistoric man and his desire to conquer the wilderness . . . ? I have *loved* (bronc riding), every single, wonderful, suffering, exhilarating, damned, blessed moment of it. . . . Pain is not too great a price to pay for the freedom of the saddle and a horse between the legs.

In 1914, Bill and Fannie launched their own small Wild West show, touring towns and cities across Montana. During these performances, Fannie got a chance to show off her skills as a sharpshooter. With a rifle, she shattered china eggs that Bill held between his fingers and knocked the ash off cigars he clenched between his teeth. Once, when trying out a new rifle, she winged Bill in the finger. He simply used another to hold the egg, so the audience wouldn't notice the miss. When Fannie nicked that finger, too, blood gushed from Bill's hand, and they cut the act short. Bill must have been relieved to skip the cigar trick.

On another occasion, Bill was thrown from a horse, knocked unconscious, and presumed dead. The show promoter frantically cast about for someone to take his place for the rest of the program and found a willing substitute in Fannie. She later explained:

> There wasn't even time for me to go to him, for I had to get ready to make his ride for him. That may seem callous, but we were show people in our own right, and "the show had to go on." I could lament for Bill later, but the horse had to be ridden right then.

Fannie retired from professional riding in 1925. She and Bill—who had survived the fall—settled on a ranch near Helmville, Montana, where they worked as outfitters, guiding hunters into the backcountry. When Bill died in 1940, Fannie continued the small business alone for another twenty-five years. She died in Helena, Montana, on February 11, 1983, at the age of ninety-five, after having been inducted into both the National Cowboy and Cowgirl halls of fame.

"If there are not horses in heaven, I do not want to go there," she once said. "But I believe there will be horses in heaven as surely as God will be there, for God loved them or He would not have created them with such majesty." ✤

JEANNETTE RANKIN

Representative for Peace

A few minutes before noon on April 2, 1917, Jeannette Rankin took a deep breath and steeled herself to make history. Clutching a bright bouquet in one hand and tucking the other under the arm of Congressman John Evans of Montana, she strode into the U.S. House of Representatives amid hearty cheers and applause. She was the first woman ever to infiltrate the sanctum of starched collars and brass spittoons—the first woman ever elected to the U.S. Congress.

The gallery was packed with people curious to see the trailblazer from Montana. One of them, the wife of a Texas representative, later recorded her impression of Jeannette's debut.

Here she was coming in, escorted by an elderly colleague, looking like a mature bride rather than a strong-minded female, and the men were clapping and cheering in the friendliest way. She wore a well-made dark-blue silk and chiffon suit, with open neck, and wide crepe collar and cuffs; her skirt was a modest walking-length, and she

MONTANA HISTORICAL SOCIETY, HELENA

Jeannette Rankin

walked well and unselfconsciously. Her hair is a commonplace brown and arranged in a rather too spreading pompadour shadowing her face. She carried a bouquet of yellow and purple flowers, given her at [a] suffrage breakfast.

She didn't look right or left until she reached her seat, far back on the Republican side, but before she could sit down she was surrounded by men shaking hands with her. I rejoiced to see that she met each one with a big mouthed, frank smile and shook hands cordially and unaffectedly. It would have been sickening if she had smirked or giggled or been coquettish; worse still if she had been masculine and hail-fellowish. She was just a sensible young woman going about her business.

Though Jeannette's first day in Congress had begun in triumph, it was destined to end in anguish. That evening, President Woodrow Wilson would ask a joint session of House and Senate to "make the world safe for democracy" by joining in the conflict that had been ravaging Europe for the past three years. He would ask Congress to declare war on Germany.

So far, the United States had remained neutral in the bloody struggle known as World War I. But in January 1917, Germany had resumed the kind of submarine warfare that had led to the sinking of the British passenger ship *Lusitania* two years earlier. Twelve hundred people had died, including 124 Americans. Now, fear of German mastery of the seas had many U.S. citizens screaming for revenge. The disclosure in March that Germany was seeking an alliance with Mexico added fuel to the fire.

The whole nation was watching the new "representative of womanhood" to see how she would answer Wilson's call to arms.

Already, Jeannette had been besieged by friends, family, and fellow lawmakers eager to help her make up her mind. Most of them advised her to do her patriotic duty and cast her vote for war, but her sister suffragists were divided. Some believed in peace at all costs, while others worried that a female vote against war would undermine the fight for women's rights. Even Jeannette's beloved brother, Wellington, pleaded with her to vote "a man's vote." To favor peace in these belligerent times, he told her, was to commit political suicide.

But Jeannette had always been repelled by the idea of war. In her view, it was a brutal, senseless way for men and nations to resolve their differences. Besides, it was bound to divert the country's energy and attention from the domestic reforms she had hoped to introduce. And she certainly was not about to send young men to their deaths just to save her seat in Congress!

The pressure was intense. Clearly, a vote for war would weigh heavy on her conscience, but a vote for peace would lose her the love and respect of people dear to her. She listened, distraught, to the House debate, hoping to find a way out of her dilemma.

By three o'clock in the morning on Good Friday, April 7, 1917, the highly charged speeches had dwindled, and the weary representatives were ready to vote. The war bill had already passed the Senate by an overwhelming margin.

The House floor was teeming and the gallery overflowing as the clerk began the roll call. As he droned on through the names in alphabetical order, many eyes focused on the "Lady from Montana." The chamber fell silent when the clerk called her name, but Jeannette didn't answer. She knew she could wait until the second roll call to cast her vote, and she wanted to postpone the painful moment for as long as possible.

The clerk began to work his way through the list of lawmakers again. This time, when her name was called, Jeannette stood and, disregarding a House rule forbidding comment during a vote, said quietly, "I wish to stand by my country, but I cannot vote for war."

Fifty-five congressmen joined Jeannette in rejecting Wilson's plea, but it was she who bore the brunt of jingoistic outrage. Press and public called her everything from traitor and coward to sentimental fool. *The New York Times* claimed her vote was proof of "feminine incapacity for straight reasoning."

"The statement she made on the floor of Congress is equal to saying 'I know what my duty is, but being a woman, I can't do it,'" concluded a state senator from Rhode Island.

Jeannette's vote for peace did as little to stop U.S. involvement in World War I as a finger in the crack of a bursting dam, but it had a big impact on her political career. As her brother had predicted, it cost her any chance at re-election in 1918, and it branded her a pacifist. But at least her conscience was clear.

"I believe that the first vote I had was the most significant vote and a significant act on the part of women," she would say years later, "because women are going to have to stop war, and I felt at the time that the first woman [lawmaker] should take the first stand— that the first time the first woman had a chance to say no to war she should say it."

Jeannette Rankin was born June 11, 1880, on a ranch six miles from Missoula, Montana Territory. She was the oldest of seven children of John Rankin, a successful rancher and building contractor, and Olive Pickering Rankin, a former schoolteacher.

The Rankins were a "forward-thinking and democratic" family, according to a Missoula teacher who knew them. They were also politically minded. John Rankin served as county commissioner for six years before dying of Rocky Mountain spotted fever in 1904. Wellington, Jeannette's only brother, would one day serve as state attorney general.

As the oldest of the Rankin offspring, Jeannette became a surrogate mother to her siblings. Her position as firstborn also helped make her a favorite with her father, who valued her opinions and encouraged her to think for herself. From him, she learned to deal with men as their equal.

Even as a girl, Jeannette proved to be resourceful and level-headed. Once, when the family dog got caught in a steel trap, she decided that the only way to save it was to amputate its paw. Not only did she perform the operation herself, but she made a leather booty to protect the animal's tender stump. On another occasion, she deftly sewed up a gash in the shoulder of her father's favorite horse.

Jeannette didn't perform as admirably in school. She found reading, writing, and arithmetic boring and as a result earned mediocre grades. But she knew she didn't want to marry and become a "perpetual baby machine" like her mother. She enrolled at the University of Montana because "it was the thing to do," and she graduated in 1902 with a degree in biology. She then tried teaching in country schools, but quit after finding the classroom just as unpleasant from the teacher's desk as it had been from the student's.

In the next few years, Jeannette toyed with the idea of becoming a seamstress or a furniture designer. She also visited relatives in Boston and San Francisco, where for the first time she witnessed the filth, poverty, and misery of the tenement slums. She was especially appalled by the plight of poor women and children, who had no political voice with which to demand a better life.

Jeannette decided to try to help the needy by becoming a social worker. After enrolling in the New York School of Philanthropy in 1908 and graduating a year later, she took a job with an orphanage in Spokane, Washington, and then another in Seattle. But she couldn't bear watching the system treat the children "like cattle." A better way to stop social injustice, she decided, was to influence legislation.

With this goal in mind, she enrolled at the University of Washington. One evening, she saw an ad in the school newspaper seeking volunteers to hang posters supporting the right of women to vote. Jeannette responded, and her career as a suffragist was launched. Through her efforts and those of other committed women, Washington in 1910 became the fifth state to approve woman suffrage—by an overwhelming margin. "I had thought the only reason wom-en didn't have the vote was because they hadn't asked for it," she later recalled.

Jeannette's efforts in Washington were not lost on the leaders of the National American Woman Suffrage Association. In 1913, the group hired her, and she spent the next two years lobbying for female suffrage in fifteen states, including Montana.

In her home state, Jeannette was named chairwoman of the Montana Woman Suffrage Association. Radiating enthusiasm and geniality, she set out on a nine-thousand-mile speaking tour, lecturing outside pool halls, at women's teas, or anywhere else she could capture an audience. Along the way, she gained valuable experience in leadership and campaigning, and her efforts helped push a suffrage amendment through the state legislature in 1913 with only two dissenting votes in each house. Montana voters—all of them men—ratified the amendment in 1914, making Montana the eleventh state to grant women the right to vote and hold public office.

But leaders of the suffrage movement still wanted victory on the national level. Jeannette recognized that it would be easier to push a suffrage bill through Congress if a woman were among its members. So she announced her candidacy for the U.S. House of Representatives. Running as a Republican, she promised to work for an eight-hour workday for women, liquor prohibition, child-welfare reform, and "preparedness that will make for peace."

Already a skilled and seasoned speaker, Jeannette once more hit the campaign trail, with her brother Wellington as adviser and financial backer. Unlike her opponents, who, she later noted, had "too much dignity," she wasn't afraid to meet the voters on their own turf—on street corners, at dance halls, in barbershops, and in lumber camps. To those who asked why a woman should sit in Congress, she replied, "There are hundreds of men to care for the nation's tariff and foreign policy and irrigation projects. But there isn't a single woman to look after the nation's greatest asset: its children."

Late on election day, November 7, 1916, Jeannette anxiously called the *Daily Missoulian* to find out how she had fared. The gruff newsman who answered the phone was frantically working on deadline and didn't yet have complete voting results. So he tossed out an answer based on his own assumption. "Oh," he said, "she lost."

Jeannette went to bed despondent and woke to headlines proclaiming her opponent's victory. Two days passed before all the votes were tallied and it became clear that Jeannette had, in fact, become the first congresswoman in U.S. history. It catapulted her into the national limelight.

"Breathes there a man with heart so brave that he would want to become one of a deliberate body made up of 434 women and himself?" the *Kentucky Courier-Journal* asked in awe.

During her first term in Congress, Jeannette sponsored legislation to aid women and children and pushed hard for a federal suffrage amendment, which was ratified in 1920. As Wellington had predicted, she lost a bid for the U.S. Senate in 1918, after pointedly campaigning to "make the world safe for humanity." But her agonizing anti-war vote, as well as the horrors of World War I, had convinced her there could be no social reform until the nation was at peace.

In May 1918, she traveled to Zurich, Switzerland, as a delegate to the Second International Congress of Women, which created the Women's International League for Peace and Freedom. The reckless slaughter of World War I spawned many peace groups, and throughout the 1920s and 1930s Jeannette was active in several of them, including the Women's Peace Union, the National Consumer's League, and the National Council for the Prevention of War.

In 1924, Jeannette bought a winter home in Georgia, a small farm with neither electricity nor plumbing. When she wasn't touring the country lobbying for peace, she lived a self-imposed Spartan existence at the farm, returning to Montana in the summer. She founded the Georgia Peace Society in 1928. It served as the hub of her peace work until its demise on the eve of World War II.

Jeannette's opposition to war grew more sophisticated in the years after her 1917 vote. She soon recognized that war stimulated the economy and would never be abolished as long as giant corporations made millions producing weapons and other supplies needed to sustain an army. She also more clearly formulated her opinion that "educating the world to peace is the women's job," saying that women were more future-oriented than men and, as mothers, could teach their children "peace habits." Because of her radical ideas, Jeannette was branded a Communist by the Atlanta post of the American Legion.

As the 1940 election neared, the rumble of guns and tanks could be heard in Europe again as Adolf Hitler invaded Poland, Denmark, Norway, Belgium, Holland, Luxembourg, and finally France. Hoping to prevent American involvement in a second world war, Jeannette filed at the last minute for another term in the U.S. House. This time her campaign slogan was "Prepare to the limit for defense, [but] keep our men out of Europe." The real enemies of the nation weren't Germany, Italy, and Japan, she argued. They were hunger, unemployment, and disease.

After twenty-two years out of the political mainstream, Jeannette once again set out to meet people in person, driving alone from one end of her congressional district to the other. She won the election, in large part because of the anti-war sentiment in the state, and once again took Montana's seat in Congress.

On December 7, 1941, Jeannette was on her way to Detroit to deliver an anti-war speech when she heard the shocking news that Japan had bombed Pearl Harbor. She rushed back to the Capitol, sure that President Franklin Roosevelt would demand a declaration of war. She must have felt an eerie sense of déjà vu the next day, as the House prepared to vote on entry into World War II. This time there was practically no debate. The wanton attack by the Japanese had galvanized public opinion, and a majority of Americans were itching to jump into battle and get revenge.

But Jeannette was just as sure about her own convictions. When the clerk called her name, she firmly answered, "Nay. As a woman I can't go to war, and I refuse to send anyone else." A stormy chorus of boos and hisses erupted in the gallery. This time, Jeannette stood alone. Hers was the only dissenting vote.

To escape her angry colleagues, as well as a barrage of flash-bulbs and reporters' questions, Jeannette stumbled to the cloakroom and barricaded herself in a phone booth. In desperation, she dialed the Capitol police and requested an escort to her office. There she was bombarded by calls, letters, and telegrams of condemnation. Even Wellington phoned to tell her that "Montana is 110 percent against you." Dismayed, Jeannette blurted, "I have nothing left now except my integrity."

Perhaps the kindest response to Jeannette's stand came from the publisher of the Kansas *Emporia Gazette*, who wrote:

Probably a hundred men in Congress would have liked to do what she did. Not one of them had the courage to do it. The *Gazette* entirely disagrees with the wisdom of her position. But, Lord, it was a brave thing! And its bravery someway discounted its folly.

When, in a hundred years from now, courage, sheer courage based upon moral indignation is celebrated in this country, the name of Jeannette Rankin, who stood firm in folly for her faith, will be written in monumental bronze not for what she did but for the way she did it.

Jeannette limped to the end of her term and returned to Georgia to lick her wounds. She did not stay there long. For the next two-and-a-half decades, she traveled the world, returning several times to India, where she hoped to meet her idol, Mohandas Gandhi, "the prophet of nonviolence." She looked forward to discussing his concept of passive resistance, but he was assassinated before she had the chance.

Jeannette resurfaced in the public eye in 1968 at the age of eighty-seven. The Vietnam War was escalating, and her desire for peace was shared now by growing ranks of anti-war protesters. On January 15, under overcast skies, nearly five thousand women marched up Louisiana Avenue to the Capitol to protest U.S. involvement in the war. They called themselves the Jeannette Rankin Brigade, and a beaming Jeannette helped carry their banner.

At the Capitol, a small delegation of women met briefly with Senator Mike Mansfield of Montana. Jeannette urged him to bring American soldiers home from Vietnam. "But how can we do this?" he politely inquired.

"The same way we got them there," the feisty crusader snapped, "by planes and ships."

As the Vietnam War dragged on, Jeannette considered running for the U.S. House again, telling a friend that she "wanted to go back to Congress to vote against a third war." But old age had finally caught up with her. A longtime throat ailment stole her voice and sidelined her with crippling pain. She died of a heart attack at a California retirement home on May 18, 1973. She was not quite ninety-three years old.

Jeannette Rankin stands out among social reformers for her dedication and endurance. She maintained an intense, often lonely struggle for peace for almost three quarters of a century, from the Progressive Era before World War I to the final hours of the Vietnam War. Although she never abandoned her ideals, she did suffer moments of doubt and despair.

"I'm a bit more frustrated now," she said wistfully, toward the end of her life. "I worked for suffrage for years and got it. I've worked for peace for fifty-five years and haven't come close."

But the measure of Jeannette's life was not her failure to abolish war. It was her honesty, integrity, conviction, and strength. Few would disagree with the college professor who once told her, "As a gallant warrior for peace and justice, a woman troubled by the tragic social ills which blight the mind and spirit of man, you give us reason to believe in the future of America." ❦

BIBLIOGRAPHY

GENERAL REFERENCES

Deutsch, Sarah. "Coming Together, Coming Apart: Women's History and the West," *Montana, the Magazine of Western History* (Spring 1991).

Faragher, John Mack. "Twenty Years of Western Women's History," *Montana, the Magazine of Western History* (Spring 1991).

Malone, Michael P., and Richard B. Roeder. *Montana: A History of Two Centuries*. Seattle: University of Washington Press, 1976.

Meyer, Annie Nathan, ed. *Woman's Work in America*. New York: Arno Press, 1972. Originally printed 1891.

Myres, Sandra L. *Westering Women and the Frontier Experience 1800-1915*. Albuquerque: University of New Mexico Press, 1982.

Petrik, Paula. *No Step Backward*. Helena: Montana Historical Society Press, 1990. Originally printed 1987.

Reiter, Joan Swallow. *The Women*, The Old West series. Alexandria, Va.: Time-Life Books, 1978.

Riley, Glenda. "Western Women's History: A Look at Some of the Issues," *Montana, the Magazine of Western History* (Spring 1991).

Scharff, Virginia. "Gender and Western History: Is Anybody Home on the Range?" *Montana, the Magazine of Western History* (Spring 1991).

Toole, K. Ross. *Montana: An Uncommon Land*. Norman: University of Oklahoma Press, 1973. Originally printed 1959.

PRETTY SHIELD

Hoxie, Frederick E. *The Crow*. New York: Chelsea House, 1989.

Linderman, Frank B. *Pretty-Shield: Medicine Woman of the Crows*. New York: The John Day Co., 1972. Originally published in 1932 as *Red Mother*.

McGinnis, Dale K., and Floyd W. Sharrock. *The Crow People*. Phoenix: Indian Tribal Series, 1972.

Merriam, Harold G. "Sign-Talker with Straight Tongue: Frank Bird Linderman," *Montana, the Magazine of Western History* (Summer 1962).

Pretty-on-Top, John (cultural director of Crow tribe). Telephone interview, April 7, 1995.

LUCIA DARLING PARK

Darling, Lucia A. Manuscript Collection 145, Montana Historical Society Archives, Helena.

"Death Came to Mrs. S. W. Park Today," *Warren Daily Tribune*, August 18, 1905.

Faust, Homer. "Montana's First School Was Taught by Miss Lucy Darling at Bannack...," Montana Newspaper Association, June 2, 1932.

"First Schools Were Missions," Montana Newspaper Association, November 8, 1937.

Not in Precious Metals Alone. Helena: Montana Historical Society Press, 1976.

Plassmann, Mrs. M. E. "First Schools in Montana Were Conducted in Private Homes," Montana Newspaper Association, April 5, 1934.

Sanders, W. F., II, and Robert T. Taylor. *Biscuits and Badmen: The Sanders Story in Their Own Words*. Butte, Mont.: Editorial Review Press, 1983.

"The Schools," *Fairfield Times*, February 17, 1927.

Thane, James L. Jr., ed. *A Governor's Wife on the Mining Frontier: The Letters of Mary Edgerton from Montana, 1863-1865*. Salt Lake City: University of Utah, Tanner Trust Fund, 1976.

Towle, Virginia Rowe. "Lucia Darling Park: Courage and Determination Behind a Demure Facade." In *Vigilante Women*. New York: A. S. Barnes & Co., 1966.

Upton, Harriet Taylor. *A Twentieth Century History of Trumbull County Ohio*. Vol. 2. Chicago: The Lewis Publishing Co., 1909.

BIBLIOGRAPHY

MATTIE CASTNER

Commager, Henry Steele. *The Great Proclamation*. New York: The Bobbs-Merrill Co., 1960.

"Death Calls J. K. Castner," *Great Falls Tribune*, December 30, 1915.

Eleventh Census of the United States. Washington, D.C.: Government Printing Office, 1895.

Great Falls Yesterday. Published by the Works Progress Administration, 1939.

Kennedy, Ethel Castner. Personal interview, October 25, 1994.

"Mattie Bost Bell Castner." Plaque in the Gallery of Outstanding Montanans, State Capitol Building, Helena. Information compiled by Montana Historical Society, 1989.

"Mother of Belt Is Dead; Was Born a Slave in South," *Great Falls Tribune*, April 3, 1920.

"Mrs. Castner Funeral Today," *Great Falls Tribune*, April 5, 1920.

Overholser, Joel. *Fort Benton: World's Innermost Port*. Privately printed, 1987.

Stober, Eva Lesell, with Ethel Castner Kennedy. *Belt Valley History, 1877-1979*. Project of Alma Chapter 110, Order of the Eastern Star, and Masonic Lodge 137, Belt, Mont., 1979.

Stout, Tom, ed. *Montana: Its Story and Biography*. The American Historical Society, 1921.

Ward, Geoffrey C., with Ric Burns and Ken Burns. *The Civil War*. New York: Alfred A. Knopf, 1990.

HELEN P. CLARKE

Clarke, Helen P. Certificate of Death, Montana Bureau of Vital Statistics.

Clarke, Helen P. "Sketch of Malcolm Clarke." In *Contributions to the Historical Society of Montana*. Vol. 2. Helena: State Publishing Co., 1896.

Ewers, John C. *The Blackfeet: Raiders on the Northwestern Plains*. Norman: University of Oklahoma Press, 1958.

Farr, William E. *The Reservation Blackfeet, 1882-1945*. Seattle: University of Washington Press, 1984.

Halligan, Rev. Father. Eulogy for Helen P. Clarke, March 7, 1923.

Hanna, Warren L. *Stars Over Montana*. Glacier National Park, Mont.: Glacier Natural History Association, 1988.

"Malcolm Clark's Daughter Was Treasure State Heroine," Montana Newspaper Association, December 11, 1939.

"Maligned by a Newspaper," *The Montana Daily Record*, September 26, 1903.

Rowell, Agnes Sherburne. "Malcom Clarke, Fur Trader, Was a Power Among Blackfeet Indians," *Great Falls Tribune*, May 15, 1932.

Turvey, Joyce Clarke. "Helen Piotopowaka Clarke." In *History of Glacier County*. Glacier County Historical Society, 1984.

MOTHER AMADEUS

Daily Yellowstone Journal, Miles City, Mont., January 19-26, 1884.

Dwyer, Sue. "Missionary Among the Indians: The Saga of Mother Amadeus," *Toledo Blade Magazine*, June 7, 1981.

"History of Religious Women in Montana." In *Religion in Montana: Pathways to the Present*. Vol. I, ed. by Lawrence F. Small. Billings, Mont.: Rocky Mountain College, 1992.

[Lincoln, Mother Angela]. *Life of the Reverend Mother Amadeus of the Heart of Jesus*. New York: The Paulist Press, 1923.

[McBride, Mother Clotilde]. *Ursulines of the West*. Mount Angel, Ore.: Mount Angel Press, 1936.

McBride, Sister Genevieve. *The Bird Tail*. New York: Vantage Press, 1974.

MARY FIELDS

Cooper, Gary (as told to Marc Crawford). "Stage Coach Mary," *Ebony Magazine* (October 1959).

"Death of Mary Fields," *Cascade Echo*, December 11, 1914.

BIBLIOGRAPHY

Harris, Mark. "The Legend of Black Mary," *Negro Digest* (August 1950).

Hutton, Charles W. "Tales of School on the Prairie in Days When Montana Was Young," *Great Falls Tribune*, November 29, 1936.

[Lincoln, Mother Angela.] *Life of the Reverend Mother Amadeus of the Heart of Jesus.* New York: The Paulist Press, 1923.

Lindesmith, Father E. W. J. Excerpts copied from his 1887 diary and kept in the archives of the Ursuline Centre, Great Falls, Mont.

McBride, Sister Genevieve. *The Bird Tail.* New York: Vantage Press, 1974.

_____. "Black Mary Labored Long at Old St. Peter's Mission," Montana Newspaper Association, August 5, 1939.

Miller, Don. "Mary Fields, Freight Hauler and Stage Driver," *True West* (August 1982).

"Nigger Mary Fields, Early Day Resident of Cascade, One of State's Noted Characters," *Great Falls Tribune*, May 22, 1939.

"Old Timer Passes Away," *Cascade Courier*, Dec. 11, 1914.

MARIA DEAN

"Board of Health," *Helena Daily Herald*, December 4, 1885.

"Dr. Maria M. Dean Dies from Illness," *Helena Independent*, May 24, 1919.

Forssen, John A., ed. *Petticoat and Stethoscope: A Montana Legend.* Missoula, Mont.: M. E. Tuchscherer, 1978.

Karolevitz, Robert F. *Doctors of the Old West.* New York: Bonanza Books, 1967.

Larson, T. A. "Montana Women and the Battle for the Ballot," *Montana, the Magazine of Western History* (Winter 1973).

Phillips, Paul C. *Medicine in the Making of Montana.* Missoula: Montana State University Press, 1962.

Vucanovich, Emily F. "The Dean Sisters," unpublished manuscript in the archives of the Montana Historical Society, Helena.

ELLA KNOWLES HASKELL

The Bates Student. Reprint of a story taken from the *Boston Transcript*, February 11, 1911.

"Ella Knowles Haskell, Well Known Lawyer, Passes Away at Butte," *Great Falls Daily Tribune*, January 28, 1911.

Haskell, Ella Knowles. "My First Fee," *Anaconda Standard*, February 3, 1907.

Progressive Men of Montana. Chicago: A. W. Bowen & Co., 1902.

Roeder, Richard B. "Crossing the Gender Line: Ella L. Knowles, Montana's First Woman Lawyer," *Montana, the Magazine of Western History* (Summer 1982).

EVELYN CAMERON

Lucey, Donna M. "Evelyn Cameron: Pioneer Photographer and Diarist," *Montana, the Magazine of Western History* (Summer 1991).

_____. "The Intimate Vision of Evelyn Cameron," *Geo* (January 1983).

_____. "Photographing Montana," *Kinesis* (1991).

_____. *Photographing Montana 1894-1928: The Life and Work of Evelyn Cameron.* New York: Alfred A. Knopf, 1990.

Naglin, Nancy. "A Montana Album," *Americana* (January/February 1991).

Taylor, Caroline. "Evelyn Cameron: Frontier Photographer," *Humanities* (October 1984).

FRA DANA

"E.L. Dana, Once Cattle King, Dies," *Great Falls Tribune*, December 15, 1946.

Ecke, Rich. "Fra Dana: Montana's Star-Crossed Impressionist," *Great Falls Tribune*, March 20, 1994.

_____. "She Was a Sophisticate, You Know," *Great Falls Tribune*, March 20, 1994.

BIBLIOGRAPHY

"Funeral Rites Friday at 2 for Mrs. Fra Dana, 74," *Great Falls Tribune*, December 2, 1948.

Kern, Dennis. "Fra Dana: Artist and Collector," brochure published by the C. M. Russell Museum, Great Falls, Mont. Revised version of brochure published by Yellowstone Art Center, Billings, Mont.

_____. Telephone interview, February 23, 1995.

FANNY CORY COONEY

Armstrong, Regina. "Representative American Women Illustrators," *The Critic* (July 1900).

Cooney, Bob, and Sayre Cooney Dodgson. "Fanny Cory Cooney: Montana Mother and Artist," *Montana, the Magazine of Western History* (Summer 1980).

Cory, Fanny Y. "My Own Story," *Indianapolis Star*, March 30, 1930.

"Fanny Cory Cooney, Nationally Known Illustrator, Will Make Her Home in Puget Sound," *Helena Independent Record*, March 21, 1954.

Firehammer, John. "The Fairy Alphabet of F. Y. Cory," *Helena Independent Record*, November 15, 1991.

King, Judy. "Fanny Cory Cooney Visiting Son and Family in Helena," *Helena Independent Record*, July 23, 1961.

Mahoney, Claude. "Indianapolis Has More Than a Reading Claim on 'Sonny,' Appearing in The Star," *Indianapolis Star*, March 30, 1930.

NANCY COOPER RUSSELL

Dippie, Brian W., ed. *"Paper Talk": Charlie Russell's American West*. New York: Alfred A. Knopf, in association with the Amon Carter Museum of Western Art, 1979.

McCracken, Harold. *The Charles M. Russell Book*. Garden City, N.J.: Doubleday & Co., 1957.

"Mrs. Russell, Widow of Cowboy Artist, Passes in California," *Great Falls Tribune*, May 25, 1940.

Renner, Ginger K. "Charlie and the Ladies in His Life," *Montana, the Magazine of Western History* (Summer 1984).

Russell, Austin. *Charlie Russell, Cowboy Artist.* New York: Twayne Publishers, 1957.

Russell-Cooper marriage announcement, *Great Falls Tribune*, September 9, 1896.

Russell, Nancy C., ed. *Good Medicine: The Illustrated Letters of Charles M. Russell.* Garden City, N.J.: Doubleday & Co., 1929.

Stauffer, Joan. *Behind Every Man: The Story of Nancy Cooper Russell.* Tulsa, Okla.: Daljo Publishing, 1990.

FANNIE SPERRY STEELE

Blakely, Reba Perry. "Wild West Shows, Rodeos and No Tears," *World of Rodeo and Western Heritage* (October 1981).

Clark, H. McDonald. "Women's Ex-Rodeo Champ Still Active at 67: Fannie Sperry Steele Operates Ranch in Blackfoot Valley," *Great Falls Tribune*, January 9, 1955.

Clark, Helen. "Fannie Sperry Steele Was a Rodeo Queen 50 Years Too Early," *Montana Farmer-Stockman*, January 21, 1965.

_____."Grand Old Lady of Rodeo: Fanny Sperry Steele," *Western Horseman* (September 1959).

_____. "Montana's Lady Rider," *Inland Empire Magazine* of *Spokesman-Review*, January 25, 1959.

Henry, Olive. "Fanny Sperry Steele Lives Alone with Her Memories," *Independent Record*, December 10, 1961.

"Horsewoman Steele Dead at 95," *Great Falls Tribune*, February 12, 1983.

Marvine, Dee. "Fannie Sperry Wowed 'Em at First Calgary Stampede," *American West* (August 1987).

Steele, Fannie Sperry. "A Horse Beneath Me . . . Sometimes," *True West* (January/February 1976).

Stiffler, Liz, and Tona Blake. "Fannie Sperry-Steele: Montana's Champion Bronc Rider," *Montana, the Magazine of Western History* (Spring 1982).

JEANNETTE RANKIN

Acceptance and Dedication of the Statue of Jeannette Rankin. Washington, D.C.: U.S. Government Printing Office, 1987.

Board, John C. "The Lady from Montana," *Montana, the Magazine of Western History* (Summer 1967).

Chamberlin, Hope. "Plight of a Dove: Jeannette Rankin, Republican of Montana." In *A Minority of Members: Women in the U.S. Congress.* New York: Praeger Publishers, 1973.

Giles, Kevin S. *Flight of the Dove: The Story of Jeannette Rankin.* Beaverton, Ore.: Touchstone Press, 1980.

Josephson, Hannah. *First Lady in Congress: Jeannette Rankin, A Biography.* Indianapolis: The Bobbs-Merrill Co., 1974.

Richey, Elinor. "Jeannette Rankin: Woman of Commitment." In *Eminent Women of the West.* Berkeley, Calif.: Howell-North Books, 1975.

Sickerman, Barbara, and Carol Hurd Green, eds. *Notable American Women: The Modern Period.* Cambridge, Mass.: The Belknap Press of Harvard University Press, 1980.

Wilson, Joan Hoff. "'Peace is a Woman's Job...' Jeannette Rankin and American Foreign Policy: The Origins of Her Pacifism," *Montana, the Magazine of Western History* (Winter, Spring 1980).

$\mathcal{I}$NDEX

HOW THE WEST WAS WON

CELEBRATE the vast spaces and rich culture of the American West. From children's books to classic western literature, from art and photography books to collections of western humor and cowboy cookbooks—brand your library in western-style with A · TWODOT · BOOK.

TO ORDER, or to request an expanded list of titles and western gift ideas, please call 1-800-582-2665, or write to Falcon, P.O. Box 1718, Helena, Montana 59624.

TWODOT